JEWS
IN TODAY'S
GERMAN CULTURE

The Helen and Martin Schwartz
Lectures in Jewish Studies, 1993

Sponsored by the
Robert A. and Sandra S. Borns
Jewish Studies Program,
Indiana University

JEWS
IN TODAY'S
GERMAN CULTURE

* * * * * * * * * * * *

Sander L. Gilman

INDIANA UNIVERSITY PRESS

Bloomington & Indianapolis

Library of Congress Cataloging–in–Publication Data

Gilman, Sander L.
    Jews in today's German culture / Sander L. Gilman.
           p. cm. — (Helen and Martin Schwartz lectures in
Jewish studies)
    Includes index.
    ISBN 0-253-32573-0
    1. German literature—Jewish authors—History and
criticism. 2. Jews—Germany—History—1945- .
3. German literature—20th century—History and criticism. 4.
Holocaust, Jewish (1939–1945) —Germany—Influence. 5. Germany—Ethnic relations. I. Title.
II. Series.
PT169.G56 1995
830.9'8924—dc20   94-18781

1 2 3 4 5 00 99 98 97 96 95

will you leaders
bleat pious laments
in the houses
where the law proclaims
freedom of a flower
to be treasured
while foul beasts
prowl the streets
defiling freedom's fruit
will hyena howls
shame your being
silence your song
homage to honour?
this time
you cannot deny
the knowing of what happens
in your midst
the third world
is aware

The South African poet James Matthews
upon visiting Frankfurt in November 1992.
(*Die Suid-Afrikaan* [May/June 1993], p. 26)

Contents

JEWS
IN TODAY'S
GERMAN CULTURE

Introduction
The Diaspora Is Not the Galut

After Auschwitz the Jewish community in Germany vanished. All followed the call of Rabbi Leo Baeck who upon his release from Theresienstadt, urged his fellow survivors to leave the land of the murderers as soon as possible. The Jewish Diaspora in the land of the murderers was at an end. Indeed, the Jewish community in Germany was pre-ordained to disappear, as its assimilation into German culture was a sign that its vanishment was a punishment for its abandonment of its traditions. The proof of this pre-ordination was the contemporaneous creation of the State of Israel. Gershom Schocken, who had been a publisher in pre-Shoah Germany, wrote in 1950 in his paper Ha'aretz *that "Israel and the World Jewish Congress have the obligation to help move the remaining Jews from Germany, so that soon no more Jews will remain there." The foundation of the State of Israel formed the basis for the gathering in of the Jews, including that remnant of German Jewry that survived the Shoah. Germany, following Hitler's and Himmler's desire, was finally "judenfrei."*

This is the common wisdom, and like most common wisdom, it is simply wrong. Jewish life in the Diaspora is particularly resilient. Indeed, the very culture of the Jewish Diaspora is a culture of rebirth and recommitment to the contradictory, double focus that any Diaspora existence presupposes.[1] To be a Jew and to be a German after the Shoah was a heightened contradiction but it was a lived, an experienced contradiction. There were and are Jews in Germany and, indeed, there is an ever growing and expanding Jewish community. More important, in the past few years what was a silent (and therefore relatively invisible) Jewish community of the victims of the Shoah has begun to reemerge as a new generation of German Jews enters into the mainstream of German cultural life. Much as the English community revived, during the centuries following the murder and the expulsion of the Jews in the Middle Ages, to become an integral part of nineteenth-century British and Jewish culture, so too the Jewish community in Germany has begun—just begun—to restructure itself as a living, integral part of both German and Jewish culture.

Now these "German" Jews—like British Jewry under Cromwell—represent a coalition of individuals from a wide range of traditions, and they all understand themselves as Jewish participants in German culture. There are Jews of Eastern European, German, and Sephardic ancestry, Jews of American ancestry only one or two generations away from their European roots, Jews who are ethnically Jewish or religiously Jewish, Jews who have discovered that one or the other parent was Jewish and have reclaimed their cultural tradition, if not their religious heritage, Jews who speak English and write German or speak German and write English, who have married into German families who were not Jewish and into German families who were Jewish, and Israeli Jews, sabras who have moved to Germany as children or as adults and who see themselves as Israelis and/or Jews in Germany. But from all these groups come players on the cultural scene. They make "art" movies (for instance, Ruth Beckermann, an Austrian Jew living in Paris, and Deborah Lefkowitz, a Jewish American film maker married to a German) or they write dramas (like the surreal dramatic exercises of Ulla Berkéwicz), or they write television shows (for example, Jurek Becker, whose "Liebling Kreuzberg" was the most popular show on German television in the 1980s, and Chantal Ackermann, whose complex visual narratives of the damaged lives of survivor children evoked the double hurt of being a woman and a child of a survivor in contemporary Europe), or novels and short stories (as is the case with the poet turned novelist Robert Schindel from Vienna; Katja Behrens, the most sophisticated "magical realist" writing in German today; and Barbara Honigmann, whose works self-consciously ignore the line between fiction and non-fiction), or they are commentators, memoirists, and interviewers (as diverse as Peter Sichrovsky, the Austrian lawyer whose interviews with the children of survivors and of the murderers have been translated into numerous languages; Chaim Noll, imprisoned in a psychiatric hospital in the German Democratic Republic because he refused to serve in the army and now a leading spokesman of the Jewish intellectuals from the former GDR; and Irene Runge, who, until the fall of the Wall was a member of the Department of Marxism-Leninism at Humboldt University in East Berlin, and who is now a leading figure in the newly unified Jewish community of "greater" Berlin).[2] All of these writers and more not only label themselves "Jews" (more or less recently), but also, in one form or another, incorporate this identity as a theme in their creative works.

In addition, there are writers on the fringe, such as the highly political poets Wolf Biermann and Günther Kunert, who articulate their "Jewish" identity only on the margins, but whose popular reception in Germany sees them as "cultural Jews."[3] Many of the women writers, like the American Jewish German-language novelist Jeannette Lander or the Austrian Jewish American German-language memoirist Ruth Klüger are also committed feminists.[4] Lander has lived in Germany for decades; Klüger, who came to the United States in 1947 after surviving Auschwitz as a child, only recently decided to return to Germany for part of each year. Lander is read by the few; Klüger's book has become a best-seller and a media sensation. In this context, the complexity of female and Jewish identity is certainly not easily resolved. Recently, Elfriede Jelinek, the most radical Austrian feminist writer and one of the best-selling novelists in Germany, announced in interviews that she *too* is Jewish—or at least has a Jewish parent. She sees herself as doubly victimized. The "dual loyalty" of Lander, Klüger, and Jelinek, to evoke one of the bugbears of Diaspora Jewish life, is to being a woman and a Jew. Yet it is also very clear that Lander, Klüger, and Jelinek inscribe their Jewishness and their femininity in very different forms in their work. For Lander they are part of the material of her fiction; for Klüger, the shaping force of her vision; for Jelinek, part of her claim for her status as a post-Shoah victim. But many non-Jewish feminists in Germany see such "divided" identities as inherently contradictory, for Judaism is, to them, the sign of the oppressor.

In the past decade, a new literature written by Jews has begun to appear in German. It represents the "negative symbiosis" of culturally embedded Jews in the new Germany.[5] This "negative symbiosis" rests on an acknowledgment of the permanent separation and simultaneous identity of Jews with Germany, especially when Germany is defined (as has been the historical pattern) in cultural terms. It also rests on a sense of sharing a common history that revolves about the Shoah but understanding this history in very different ways. This "negative symbiosis" is in no way a mind-set that has developed among Jews in Germany since 1989, the date of the creation of the "new" Germany. But it began to be articulated in the late 1980s within the world of culture in a complex manner by a relatively large number of self-identified Jewish cultural figures. It is not just that these figures are "Jewish" (however that term comes to be used), it is that the very question of what it means to be "Jewish" in today's Germany, the Germany of this new generation, comes to be the theme of their work.

These writers feel themselves to be part of, yet alienated from, this new Germany. They live in what used to be the German Democratic Republic, in what is still the Federal Republic of Germany, or in Austria. Some of them, such as Becker and Noll, had broken with the traditions of the GDR and had been harshly treated by its authorities. To them can be added Thomas Brasch, a Jew expelled from the German Democratic Republic in 1976 and now living in London.[6] For them, the fall of the Wall provided some sense of justification for their opposition and sharpened their sense of what it meant to be "Jewish" in a new Germany. For others, such as Beckermann and Schindel with their Austrian background, this world historical event that seemed to mark the end of history (at least in the thoughts of the mayor of West Berlin the morning after the wall was opened) had relatively little impact, while the opening to Eastern Europe, to the world once inhabited by the largest single settlement of Jews in the world, evoked many new sensations and feelings.

However, this literature is marked not only by the expected line of demarcation between the "German" (or the "Austrian") and the "Jew" (while drawing that boundary into question) but also clearly by the gender of the author. As we shall see, the meaning of the gendered body comes to have a central role in defining the meaning of the "negative symbiosis" of the Jew in Germany.

Comprehending the complexities of a Jewish cultural life in Germany since 1945 or, even more, since 1989, means understanding the complexities of these models of self-representation of Jewish existence in "exile." These models of the "exile of the Jews," of the "nation within a nation," exist both within Judaism as a religion and a culture as well as beyond the Jewish community in the various cultures in which Jews live. Christian and Islamic communities, since both need to make the Jews visible in their own way, promulgate a special sense of the presence of the Jews in "exile." As long as the "exile" was a conceptual one—as long as there was no "there" for the Jews except in the abstract textual sense of the historic space of the Jews as represented in the Torah—this problem was not acute. The "exile" of the Jews was the real world experience of Jewry even in the outer reaches of the traditional lands of the Jews, and it could be overcome only by the promised coming of the Messiah and the ingathering of the Jews. Political Zionism and the formation of the state of Israel fulfilled this goal before the end of history. "Aliyah," a going-up to the state of Israel, was a dogma of the new Diaspora; no one could imagine "Yeridah," a going-down from Israel, a return into the Diaspora, for example, to Germany. And yet it is precisely this world of Diaspora Judaism in Germany, now replenished by Jews from throughout the world, to which one can turn to examine the resuscitation of a Jewish culture in the Diaspora.

One of the great problems Jews and non-Jews have had since the founding of the state of Israel is understanding Jewish life beyond Israel or the Holy Land as a valid life experience. Since the founding of the state of Israel, "exile" has meant exile from a real, geographically bounded place, while the act of returning, endlessly postponed, is now a possibility. The traditional models of the "exile" experience of Jews, especially Jews in the special circumstances of Germany, still provide a good way to understand this Jewish experience.

The contradictory yet overlapping models of a Jewish "Diaspora," as opposed to a Jewish "Galut," have formed the Jewish self-understanding of what "exile" means. The voluntary dispersion of the Jews ("Galut" or "Golah") is understood as inherently different from the involuntary exile of the Jews ("Diaspora"). These two models exist simultaneously in Jewish history in the image of rooted and empowered Jews on the one hand, and uprooted and powerless Jews on the other. It is possible to have a firm, meaningful cultural experience as a Jew in the Diaspora or to feel alone and abandoned in the Galut (and vice versa)—two people can live in the very same place and time and can experience that place and time in antithetical ways. Indeed, the same person can find his or her existence bounded conceptually by these two models at different times and in different contexts.

The notion of a dispersion of the Jews is inscribed in the Torah in a specific manner with negative, punishing overtones. The dispersion represents a punishment for the transgression of particular boundaries. The idea of a textual model for the Diaspora rooted in the Torah and reflected in other writings is important to any understanding of a Jewish articulation of the meaning of "exile." But the very assumption of the Diaspora is ambiguous and contradictory, even though it carries the force of divine revelation incorporated in texts. The Galut, on the other hand, is often understood as the experienced reality of being in exile, structured, however, by the internalization of the textual notion of the Diaspora tempered by the daily experience (good or bad) of life in the world. The Jew experiences the daily life of "exile" through the mirror of the biblical model of the expulsion—whether it be the expulsion from the Garden of Eden or captivity in Egypt. If these two experiences are parallel—if life in the Galut is harsh and painful (as it often was), it seems a further proof of the validity of the model of the Diaspora. The South African Jewish writer Sandra Braude has stated this succinctly: "But Jews tend to forget that there is only one promised land, and that they seldom are permitted to remain in any one place for longer than three generations."[7] If Jewish experience is contradictory to the expectations of the "Diaspora" model, as in the "Golden Age" of the Jews in Spain or the "exile" of Jews in the United States, the meaning of the models becomes muddled. Germany after the Shoah seems to present both possibilities. First it was the ultimate trial of the Diaspora Jew—the *Churban*, the murder of the Six Million—but now it represents a modern, democratic/socialist state (or states), clearly different from, but still the same as the Germany of the past. Here the question of geography becomes central—is this "new" living space, the new Germany (especially after the creation of yet another "new" Germany in 1989), a place where Jews should live? That they do live there goes without question.

The biblical or textual model of the Diaspora centers around a geography that defines Jewish identity.[8] The Jews are a chosen people with a divinely chosen land and exile is a recurrent state that must be resolved by a return to that chosen land. Thus, within the Torah there is an established textual tradition of the Diaspora. Exile in Egypt comes to serve as the ideal model for Babylonian exile, which in turn comes to serve as a model for the exile from Spain and Portugal, which in turn. . . . But Egypt was both a voluntary outgoing from the Holy Land, an experience of mutual benefit (cultural symbiosis) for Jews and Egyptians, as well as a cruel incarceration (a true Diaspora). The only answer for this series of false human steps that drew the Jews away from the Holy Land into the land of Egypt was divine redemption and the punishment of the "Hosts of Egypt," who attempted to stop the Jews from leaving their Diaspora. These "hosts" violated their guests' *heimarmene*, the comfort always offered the stranger. The cruelty of the Egyptians was a breach of friendship, the transformation of a Galut experience into a Diaspora experience. And in the textual model, the Galut experience, the peaceful going out from the appropriate place for the Jews into the world, is transformed into the torment of slavery, of death, of loss of faith in the Egyptian Diaspora.

God promised the patriarchs that their children would be "as the dust of the earth: so that if a man can number the dust of the earth, so shall thy seed be numbered" (Gen. 13:16). But the Diaspora reading of that promise is tinged with the bitterness of exile: "As the dust of the earth is scattered from one end of the world to the other thus your children will be scattered from one end of the world to the other, as the dust of the earth causes even metal vessels to wear out but exists for ever, so Israel is eternal but the nations of the world will come to naught . . . as the dust of the earth is threshed, so thy children will be threshed by the nations . . ." (Gen. R. 41:9). Here the promise of fecundity is linked to the curse of "exile" in the sense of the Diaspora.

The Assyrian (722 B.C.E.) and Babylonian (597 B.C.E.) Diaspora were textually represented as very similar. Corruption in Israel became the rationale for the prediction of Nebuchadnezzar's capture of Jerusalem and his destruction of the Temple. Jeremiah's description of the Babylonian enslavement was cast in terms of the Diaspora. The appropriate punishment was exile from the land of Israel. And redemption means return: "I will gather you from all the nations, and from all the places whither I have driven you" (Jer. 29:14). And for Jeremiah, the promise of redemption is real: "After seventy years be accomplished at Babylon I will visit you, and perform my good word toward you, in causing you to return to this place" (Jer. 29:10). Ezekiel makes a similar promise: "Yet will I leave a remnant, that ye may have some that shall escape the sword among the nations, when ye shall be scattered through the countries" (Ezek. 6:8). It is of little wonder that the survivors of the Shoah, living in displaced persons camps in Germany, came to speak of themselves as the "She'erit ha-Peletah," the surviving fragment, the term for those who survived the Babylonian captivity and eventually returned to Jerusalem. The biblical model comes to define the Jewish experience as an experience in exile. Jeremiah, like Ezekiel, expressed nostalgia for the days of the Exodus and the Wilderness, and this view is seen as having been incised onto the body of the Jew in the form of circumcision. As we shall see, this theme, the different body of the Jew among the bodies of those Others among whom they live, comes to be a central trope in the working out of the notion of a Jewish identity in contemporary Germany. To understand its power it is necessary to comprehend its textual roots.

How will the Jews be set apart from all other peoples? For Jeremiah, the special nature of the Jewish body will set them apart in the Diaspora. It is the covenant inscribed on the body of the male Jew, in the very act of circumcision, which makes the Jew different and separate. The Jewish people will never become like the other nations. "Circumcise yourselves to the Lord, and take away the foreskins of your heart . . ." he calls out (Jer. 4:4) and threatens in turn, "I will punish all of them which are circumcised with the uncircumcised" (Jer. 9:25). It is the alteration of the spirit to represent the difference of the body that Jeremiah demands of the Jews in the Diaspora. This theme haunts the discourse of the textually determined reading of the Diaspora in Jeremiah and Ezekiel.[9]

All (male) Jews are physically the same. Circumcision is the sign of the covenant in Genesis. And circumcision is associated with the Egyptian Diaspora in Exodus. Moses is symbolically circumcised in Midian when he is called to return to Egypt to free his people. His wife, Zipporah, circumcises their son with a "sharp stone" to save Moses from God's wrath—a "bloody husband art thou, because of the circumcision" (Exod. 4:23-26). Later, at the Passover meal, Moses is ordered to admit the circumcised servants and strangers (Exod. 12:43-48): "When a stranger shall sojourn with thee and will keep the Passover to the Lord, let all his males be circumcised"; these people are then brought out of the land of Egypt. The inscription of the body sets the Jews apart in the Diaspora.[10]

By the nineteenth century, this notion comes to mark the Jew's body as unchanging and separate. In Richard Andree's 1881 study of Jewish folklore, the central question is the relationship between ideas of who the Jews are and what their bodies mean. Andree's discussion centers on the permanence of the Jewish racial type, but more important, on its implications. Andree is the most widely cited German expert who argued for the immutability of the Jew. He was a strong advocate of the view that the Jews were a pure (but defective) race. He observed, concerning the conservative nature of the Jewish body and soul:

> No other race but the Jews can be traced with such certainty backward for thousands of years, and no other race displays such a constancy of form, none resisted to such an extent the effects of time, as the Jews. Even when he adopts the language, dress, habits, and customs of the people among whom he lives, he still remains everywhere the same. All he adopts is but a cloak, under which the eternal Hebrew survives; he is the same in his facial features, in the structure of his body, his temperament, his character.[11]

And the body of the Jew is the sign of this immutability. In 1902 the debate about the immutability of the Jew was again raised in the public press when the professor of archeology at the University of Berlin, Friedrich Delitzsch, delivered his lecture on "Babel and Bible" before Emperor Wilhelm II.[12] Delitzsch argued that the Assyrian excavations being undertaken at the time were important for understanding the background of biblical history. He also argued, with telling visual images from Babylonian sources, that it was quite possible to distinguish the image of the Jews as depicted on these ancient monuments because of similarities in appearance to Wilhelmenian images of the Jews. Delitzsch's presentation caused an uproar because of his visual "proof" of the immutability of the Jewish body.

In the Diaspora, the negative experiences of the Jews makes the integral and identifiable nature of the Jew's body central to any understanding of the Jew's difference. The Jews articulate their difference in terms of their body, as do those opposed to their presence in the Diaspora. And each can call upon textual evidence, from the "Book," for their proof. The "Jews," as seen from the perspective of those objecting to the Jewish presence in the world of the Diaspora, are inherently different; Jews present physical difference based on the practice of infant male circumcision as a sign of their difference from others within the Diaspora.

The alternative model is that of the Jewish body in the Galut. The Jews are ubiquitous and are inherently nomadic, according to Andree's model. Their presence throughout the world is a result of their perverse desire to be out of their "appropriate" land. There is no land without its Jews in this model. As early as the second century B.C.E., the Hellenistic Sibylline oracle could sing that "Every land is full of you, and every sea" but also that "it is thy fate to leave thine holy soil" (Or. Sibyl. 3:267). In the first century, the Greek historian Strabo stated that there was not a place in the entire world into which the Jewish nation had not penetrated. And by the second half of the first century, it was stated that "among every nation are the dispersed of Israel according to the word of God" (Ps. of Sol. 9:2). By the nineteenth century, Jewish communities could be found in China, India, and Africa as well as throughout those lands colonized by the European powers.

And these Jews are seen as economically, culturally, and socially successful in this context, in spite of the oppression they encountered. Franz Kafka spoke of the power given to the Jews in this struggle for survival:

> The Jewish people is scattered, as a seed is scattered. As a seed of corn absorbs matter from its surroundings, stores it up, and achieves further growth, so the destiny of the Jews is to absorb the potentialities of mankind, purify them, and give them a higher development. Moses is still a reality. As Abiram and Dathan opposed Moses with the words *"Lo naale!* We will not go up!" so the world opposes him with the cry of anti-Semitism. In order not to rise to the human condition men sink into the dark depths of the zoological doctrine of race. They beat the Jews and murder humanity.[13]

The Jews integrated themselves to one degree or another into Galut culture and yet are seen and see themselves as separate from that culture because of the power of the Diaspora model, the biblical model of exodus and dispersion. The anxiety is that there will be a loss of religious or ethnic center through acculturation or assimilation, and loss comes to be inscribed on the body.

In the 1920s, Jacob Wassermann chronicled the ambivalence of the German Jews toward their own bodies, their own difference. Wassermann articulates this difference in terms of the biology of race. He writes: "I have known many Jews who have languished with longing for the fair-haired and blue-eyed individual. They knelt before him, burned incense before him, believed his every word; every blink of his eye was heroic; and when he spoke of his native soil, when he beat his Aryan breast, they broke into a hysterical shriek of triumph."[14] Their response, Wassermann argues, is to feel disgust for their own bodies, which even when identical in *all* respects to the those of the Aryans remains different: "I was once greatly diverted by a young Viennese Jew, elegant, full of suppressed ambition, rather melancholy, something of an artist, and something of a charlatan. Providence itself had given him fair hair and blue eyes; but lo, he had no confidence in his fair hair and blue eyes: in his heart of hearts he felt that they were spurious."[15]

Jews are physically different and yet they are the same. Werner Sombart, in *The Jews and Modern Capitalism*, provides a clear image of the Jewish body as a sign of its adaptability (which is a sign of its inherent immutability):

> The driving power in Jewish adaptability is of course the idea of a purpose, or a goal, as the end of all things. Once the Jew has made up his mind what line he will follow, the rest is comparatively easy, and his mobility only makes his success more sure. How mobile the Jew can be is positively astounding. He is able to give himself the personal appearance he most desires. . . . The best illustrations may be drawn from the United States where the Jew of the second or third-generation is more difficultly distinguished from the non-Jew. You can tell the German after no matter how many generations; so with the Irish, the Swede, the Slav. But the Jew, in so far as his racial features allow it, has been successful in imitating the Yankee type, especially in regard to outward marks such as clothing, bearing and the peculiar method of hairdressing.[16]

By the latter half of the nineteenth century, Western European Jews had become indistinguishable from other Western Europeans in matters of language, dress, occupation, location of their dwellings, and the cut of their hair. Indeed, if Rudolf Virchow's extensive study of over 10,000 German school children published in 1886 is accurate, they were also indistinguishable in terms of skin, hair, and eye color from most of those who lived in Germany.[17] Virchow's statistics sought to show that wherever a greater percentage of the overall population had lighter skin or bluer eyes or blonder hair, a greater percentage of Jews there also had lighter skin or bluer eyes or blonder hair. But although Virchow attempted to provide a rationale for the sense of Jewish acculturation, he still assumed that Jews were a separate and distinct racial category. George Mosse has commented, "the separateness of Jewish schoolchildren, approved by Virchow, says something about the course of Jewish emancipation in Germany. However rationalized, the survey must have made Jewish schoolchildren conscious of their minority status and their supposedly different origins."[18] Nonetheless, even though they were labeled as different, Jews came to parallel the scale of types found elsewhere in European society.

The sense of the difference of the Jewish body remained prevalent among Jews even under the pressure of heightened anti-Semitism in the 1930s. Political awareness in no way mitigated the notion that the permanence of the Jew's face marked the inherent difference between the Jew and the Aryan. In 1924, the eponymous heroine of Arthur Schnitzler's *Fräulein Else*, a young girl about to be sacrificed to an older man to aid her bankrupt father, comments to herself on the art dealer to whom she is about to be sold: "You might as well be an old-clothes man as an art dealer—But, Else Else, what makes you say a thing like that?—O, I can permit myself a remark of this sort. Nobody notices it in me. I'm even blonde, a strawberry blonde, and Rudi [her brother] looks absolutely like an aristocrat. Of course, one can notice it easily in Mother, especially in her speech, but not at all in Father. Really they ought to notice it in me. More than that—let them notice it."[19] The "it," of course, is the hidden taint, the visible invisibility of the Jewishness of her parents. In Schnitzler's world one could always tell who is a Jew, as the simple-minded Aryan *Leutnant* Gustl comments to himself at the theater: "They say the Mannheimers themselves are Jews, baptized, of course . . . they don't look it—especially Mrs. Mannheimer . . . blond, beautiful figure."[20] The Jewish poet, Georg Mannheimer, writing in exile in Prague in 1937, could evoke the "strange face" of the Jew:

> I know: you don't love us.
> We are not like the others.
> People who rest and people who wander
> Have a totally different face.
>
> I know: you don't love us.
> We have swum through too many streams.
> But, let us come to rest,
> Then we shall have the same face.[21]

Mannheimer's poem evokes the notion of the potential elimination of any "ugliness" associated with the "nomadic" nature ascribed to the Jew. Here it is not evolution but acculturation that will alter the internalized sense of alienation that marks the face of the Jew.

A parallel shift in the perception of the Jewish body can be found during the twentieth century in the United States. In 1910 the famed German Jewish anthropologist and founder of modern American anthropology, Franz Boas, wrote a detailed report for Congress on the "Changes in Bodily Form of Descendants of Immigrants."[22] This report documented the change in body size, cephalic index, even hair color, of the offspring of Jewish, Sicilian, and Neapolitan immigrants born in the United States. Unlike their siblings born abroad, first-generation immigrants were bigger, had greater brain capacity, and lighter hair color. Boas attempted to argue that racial qualities, even the color of the hair, change when the environment shifts and that racial markers are, at least to some degree, mutable. Needless to say, this view was contested in the science of his time. Arguments against this view ranged from seeing the change as the impact of the shift from rural to urban life in America to seeing it as a true reversal of the "degenerate" types which developed in Europe under capitalism and thus the reemergence of the "pure" and therefore healthier original European types. The idea that there could be a "new human race" evolving under American conditions startled European scientists. But these Eastern European Jewish immigrants were not only physically becoming more and more like other Americans, they were also growing into American culture.[23] As the body type altered, their culture also changed.

Not only do second- and third-generation descendants of East-ern European Jewish immigrants not "look" like their grandparents, they "look" American. The writer and director Philip Dunne com-mented on the process of physical acculturation of Jews in southern California during the twentieth century:

> You could even see the physical change in the family in the sec-ond generation–not resembling the first generation at all. Of course, this is true all across the country, but it is particularly no-ticeable in people who come out of very poor families. . . . One dear friend and colleague of mine was a product of a Lower East Side slum. He was desperately poor. And he grew up a rickety, tiny man who had obviously suffered as a child. At school, he told me, the goyim would scream at him. Growing up in Califor-nia, his two sons were tall, tanned, and blond. Both excelled aca-demically and in athletics. One became a military officer, the other a physicist. They were California kids. Not only American but Californian.[24]

But the more the Jews in Germany and Austria at the fin de siècle looked like their non-Jewish contemporaries, the more they sensed themselves as different and were so considered. As the Anglo-Jewish social scientist Joseph Jacobs noted in the late nineteenth century, "it is some quality which stamps their features as distinctly Jewish. This is confirmed by the interesting fact that Jews who mix much with the outer world seem to lose their Jewish quality. This was the case with Karl Marx. . . ."[25] And yet, as we know, it was precisely those Jews who were the most assimilated, passing as non-Jews, who feared that their visibility as Jews could come to the fore. It was they who most feared being seen as bearing that disease, Jewishness, which the mid-nineteenth-century German Jewish poet Heinrich Heine said the Jews brought from Egypt. For Heine, too, in his me-morial of the German Jewish writer Ludwig Börne, it is the body, specifically the "long nose that is a type of uniform, by which the King-God Jehovah recognizes his old retainers, even if they have deserted."[26]

In this model of the Galut, the body changes and adapts and yet reveals itself; in the model of the Diaspora, it remains unchang-

ing and marked. This tension exists for each Jew self-consciously.
Am I the same as all others or am I a Jew or am I both simultaneously? This double bind is reflected in the general lack of stability
that Jewish writers sense in their cultural position in the Diaspora/
Galut. Tracing this complex in the presence of younger Jews in German culture means trying to understand their cultural position,
which is the purpose of the first chapter. The second chapter is dedicated to a close analysis of the critical reception of two of the younger
generation's most interesting writers and thus an analysis of their
audiences. The German situation today, as we shall see, provides a
heightened context for feelings of invisibility (being seen as all others) or visibility (being seen as different from all others), which form
a theme that literally becomes inscribed in the representation of the
Jewish body in contemporary German Jewish culture. This theme is
treated in the final chapter. This book is a first attempt to understand the complexities of a very recent and still evolving development. Though tentative, this formulation will, I hope, provide some
insight into the complexities of life in the present-day German Galut.

Jewish Self-Consciousness and Awareness of Jews in Post-Wall Germany

When I was in high school and at the university, one of the very few literary works read in the classroom which dealt with the Jews in Germany—besides *Nathan the Wise*—was a classic novella by the Biedermeier poet Annette von Droste-Hülshoff. Called "The Jews' Beech," it recounted the tale of the murder of a Jewish peddler and the fate of his murderer. The murder takes place under a beech tree and the Jewish community asks permission to preserve the site. They inscribe upon the tree a line of badly garbled Hebrew which remains untranslated until the end of the story:

Im tiamod bamekom hazeh yifka buch k'asher atat asita lo

The murderer, horribly mutilated after decades in slavery in North Africa, eventually returns to the small Westphalian town, where he goes unrecognized, and at the end hangs himself on the "Jews' Beech." In the very last line of the story, we learn that the Hebrew words cut into the Jews' beech tree mean "If you approach this place, you will suffer what you inflicted on me."[1]

This story had etched itself into my memory, because, unlike the kind and benign (if sterile) figure of Nathan the Wise, there was something vaguely threatening about the power of Droste-Hülshoff's Jews, who are represented only as an ever-growing collective. Their seemingly mystical means of drawing the criminal back to the site of his crime and his self-imposed retribution relied on the murderer's gnawing guilt rather than on Jewish vengeance. Yet there was literally a magical presence in the tale when I read it, represented in the appearance on the page (printed in Gothic script) of the "straight lines and curved lines and dots" of the Hebrew alphabet, to use the image that Philip Roth associates with his fantasy of the emblematic Jewish writer in German, Franz Kafka.[2] All alphabets, the Hebrew and German alphabets included, according to Roth's Kafka, are really just "straight lines and curved lines and dots." And yet the use of the Hebrew alphabet gives magical meaning to the prophecy of Droste-Hülshoff's Jews when it appears carved into the Jews' beech tree, like the Hebrew that adorned Renaissance amulets in Germany.

After the fall of the Wall, the German government changed its currency and dedicated the most widely circulated—the twenty mark bill—to the memory of Annette von Droste-Hülshoff. (The plan to alter the currency was actually formulated prior to German reunification, but the change actually occurred some six months after reunification and came to be associated with that historical moment.) Along with Clara Schumann, this acknowledgment of the role played by women in German culture was a "liberal" gesture in the iconography of the world of capital. And yet this liberal gesture had an odd twist to it. On the reverse of the bill is a circle in which the ghost of the "Jews' Beech" evokes Droste-Hülshoff's best-known prose work—but it is an odd beech tree, given the novella, since the defacement that marks it (and the tale) is missing. It is a Jew's beech without the magical Hebrew letters.

The evocation of the tale by the representation of the beech tree represses the signification of the tree. The Jewish script has vanished as if it never existed and the eerie presence of the Jews in the story has vanished along with it. And this is understandable, for the very evocation of a beech tree after the Shoah evokes that very special beech tree, Goethe's beech tree, which stood at the center of the concentration camp at Buchenwald. Droste-Hülshoff's beech only has meaning with its Hebrew inscription and yet a Hebrew inscription on a beech gracing a piece of German currency would carry too many other associations. This simultaneous presence and absence, this evocation and repression of the acknowledgment and visibility of the Jews in post-Wall Germany, are central to those young writers who understand themselves today as Jewish writers there.[3] Jews in contemporary reunited Germany, the Germany after the Wall, come to acknowledge their simultaneous visibility and invisibility, their sense of belonging along with their sense of difference, and represent this ambiguity in their literary work. Although not necessarily a result of the fall of Communism and the reunification of the two German states, the situation is heightened by this historical context. The growth of a new Jewish culture in all of Germany would have taken place without the fall of the Wall, but it certainly would have taken a different form and direction. The sense of being "integrated foreign bodies" ("integrierter Fremdkörper"), as the Jewish novelist Esther Dischereit has her protagonist describe herself at the close of her recent novel *Merryn* (1992), does not come from political changes.[4] What is different is the cultural context in which these young Jewish writers now begin to articulate their sense of belonging and yet not belonging.

This is why Dan Diner, the most articulate social critic from within the Jewish intellectual community in Germany, has labeled this state of mind a "negative symbiosis."[5] Accepting, on one level, Gershom Sholem's dismissal of the "German-Jewish symbiosis" as a fantasy on the part of Jews in Germany before the Shoah, Diner asks how Jews can live in Germany today. His answer—and as we shall see, it is an answer that articulates the problem rather than exemplifying the models of resistance that make Jewish culture possible in contemporary Germany—is that Jews exist in a "negative symbiosis" with German culture, aware of and forced to deal with their own difference from the "German." Thus Rafael Seligmann, taking the American case as exemplary, can write about the Jews in Germany as the "Indians of Germany," in analogy to the status of the "vanished American" who is not black (like the "real" minority) in the United States and who are present more in myth than in reality.[6] But their notion of "Germany" is defined in terms of their self-identified Jewishness. It comes to be the antithesis or extension of their understanding of the Jew. Thus their Germany is peopled by "Germans"—a rather risky generalization given the fact that there

are over a million and a half people of Turkish descent in contemporary Germany who may or may not be included in any legal definition of the "German" but who certainly complicate the simple dichotomy of "German" and "Jew." And, as we shall see, it is this
complexity that makes the new visible invisibility of the Jew in German culture possible.

There is also a sense of the complexity of the relationship these
writers have to their audiences in Germany. Obviously, the greater
reading and viewing audience is non-Jewish, and yet it has a very
special relationship to things "Jewish." But in addition there exists
an internal, Jewish audience in Germany for or against which these
writers often define themselves. Jewish journals such as the muck-
raking *Semit-Times,* and the intellectual *Babylon,* the student journals
such as *Tachles* (in Frankfurt) or *Nudnik* (in Munich), official or
quasi-official newspapers of the Jewish communities, such as the
Frankfurt Jewish News or the *General Paper of the Jews in Germany,* provide a Jewish response to writers who represent Jewish life in contemporary Germany. Writers respond to an audience that sees them
as Jewish because they have chosen to label themselves Jews and to
write on themes involving *contemporary* Jewish life. Their non-Jewish
audience "sees" them as representative Jews; their Jewish audience
often sees this heightened visibility as potentially dangerous. How
complicated this response becomes can be judged from the overall
problem of the intense visibility of the Jews (however defined) in
contemporary Germany, coupled with their inherent invisibility.

This ambiguity measures itself against the sense of Jews as different that has developed in today's Germany.[7] The commission on
constitutional reform of the upper house of parliament, the
Bundesrat, decided on May 14, 1992, that a clause regarding "national and ethnic minorities" should be included in the revision of
the constitution or Basic Law and should "specifically apply to the
Danish, Sorb, and Frisian populations, the German Sinti and Roma
(Gypsies), and—as far as a specific sense of themselves as a minority
("ein entsprechendes Minderheitenselbstverständnis") exists—the
Jewish population."[8] Jews are both a "minority" and not a "minority," while the other groups are distinctly minorities. The old,

unresolvable questions of what is a Jew—a member of an ethnic, social, cultural, "racial," or religious group—may lie obliquely behind this bracketing of Jewish identity in Germany. But also, clearly, the unique sense of a lost joint history, a history that encompasses both the Enlightenment promise of the identification of Jews as Germans and the Nazi reversal of this promise, lies behind it as well. The Jews are not like other minority or "out" groups in Germany. And yet all are defined in terms of a static, homogeneous image of the "center," of the German. This notion of being German as becoming something different from what one senses oneself to be lies at the very heart of the literary self-representation of the Jewish writer in Germany.

Perhaps the best example of this ambiguity is the dilemma of the Sinti and the Roma, the Gypsies, as represented in the discussions about the nature of foreigners prior to the changes of the constitutional right of asylum in July 1993. This is a group that also suffered in the Shoah but one for whom there was never the implicit promise of cultural identification as "Germans." In July 1992, Romani Rose, the chair of the central committee of the German Sinti and Roma, published a moving call to fulfill the German government's pledge that the German Gypsies have a status equal to that of other "national and ethnic minorities" in Germany.[9] Rose was referring to the intense hatred and violence, the 2,427 "criminal acts against foreigners" in 1991 and the even greater number carried out in 1992. This was a marked increase from the 246 crimes of this nature in 1990.[10] The incidents of racially motivated murder, beatings, and arson were carried out by a relatively small number of right-wing hate-mongers in all areas of the Federal Republic of Germany during 1992, and many of them were directed against "visible foreigners," political asylum seekers, as well as any others who looked or were perceived to look different. This includes gays, lesbians, and the handicapped.

Central to Rose's concern was certainly the campaign of vilification aimed at the some 30,000 Romanian Gypsies who, once they could, fled from persecution and "Romanianization." Since November 1992, their potential mass expulsion from Germany has been a measurable fact. The German Federal government offered a compelling deal to the new government of Romania to accept back into the country those "undocumented" citizens who could be identified as Romanian. And in this context, Romanian is understood as Gypsy. This deal was struck in the light of the Nazi murder of more than 500,000 Romany and of the long-standing animosity and ongoing persecution of the Gypsies by Romanian nationalists.

The theoretical expulsion of the Sinti and Roma violated the spirit, if not the letter, of the German Basic Law's standard of asylum before July 1, 1993, a right built into this law by those aware of the great number of refugees from Germany denied asylum throughout the world during the 1930s and 1940s. Indeed, very few of them were expelled immediately following November 1992, as those at risk quietly vanished into the vast undocumented underground of illegal aliens. During the first four months of 1993, 161,000 asylum seekers arrived in the Federal Republic, with the greatest number coming from Romania. But by the beginning of August, 1993, shortly after the revision of Article XVI of the Basic Law, which took effect on July 1, a plane load of deportees every day was being returned to the "safe" haven of Romania.[11] The debate about the Sinti and Roma in 1992 did produce a discussion in the following months with the "neighboring" states to the east of the Federal Republic, such as Poland and the Czech Republic, with the agreement that they would accept the deportation of asylum seekers attempting to reach Germany via a third country. In May 1993, Germany signed an agreement with Poland to accept 10,000 illegal immigrants who came from or who had passed through Poland on their way to the Federal Republic. This number will be unlimited in 1994. And, one might add, an aide to the German Federal Chancellor acknowledged the "special responsibility" that the German government felt toward the Romany.[12] The sense of the moment was that the Germans had "lost control over what was happening to them," and that the "politicians picked up the anxieties of the people and carried them one step further," according to Ruprecht von Arnim from the office of the United Nations Commissioner for Refugees in Brussels.[13]

Yet the response to the increased migration of Gypsies (and other asylum seekers) to Germany was to see in them a danger to the state and to attempt to expel them or to bar their entry. The unofficial response was to burn them out of their temporary refuges. The official response seems to support the contention of the editorial writer of the *Washington Post* that "if you don't like the behavior of the people next door—how they look, smell, dress—and you aren't satisfied with the official response, the way to get quick government action is to attack these people physically and firebomb their houses. At that point the government will do what you wanted all along—get rid of them."[14] And it was indeed the sense that the Gypsies were "different," that they could not be assimilated in any way, which lay behind their being targeted as undesirable by the mobs and the government. And this difference is defined in the New Europe through the visibility of the foreigner, as Zoubida Djelali, an Algerian doctor, observed: "The police already stop foreigners—they do it all the time now. They just go by the color of the face."[15]

The Jews in Germany are in a very different situation. Certainly by the 1990s, even the Eastern Jews who settled in Germany as "displaced persons," their children, and their grandchildren had become thoroughly acculturated to German social norms. They did not look, smell, or dress differently, even if, following the Shoah, the myth of their physical difference was popularly perpetuated. The Sinti and Roma and the Turks, in their visibility (from the standpoint of the "Germans") make the Jews, even new immigrants, less visible. Indeed, the very number of Turks in Germany (now 1.8 million), many of them born there, marks them as visible. The Jews are seen and yet not seen; present and yet invisible. Even the great mass of Soviet Jews who were actively leaving the former USSR were seen as a potentially desirable minority, at least by the left. At a lecture at Cornell in November 1992 by a German academic specialist in German immigration politics, "highly educated" Russian Jews were labeled assimilable, because they looked like Germans and could easily learn the German language. But the treatment of this cohort of Jews was still very different from that accorded the "ethnic Germans" being repatriated from the former USSR. Daniel Cohn-Bendit, himself Jewish, demanded at an open-air meeting on Jewish immigration in Frankfurt in May 1990 that Russian Jews of "German ancestry" be treated identically to the ethnic Germans being repatriated from the then USSR. This was greeted with loud approval by his partisan audience.[16] (Ironically, by early 1993, the German government had begun to finance the resettlement of some of these Germans in their pre-1941 lands along the Volga so as to preclude their claiming their German citizenship under the *lex sanguinis,* the law of blood relationship, which makes them de facto German citizens.)

Turks were and are seen as unassimilable, even though writers such as Zehra Cirak and Aras Ören are now permanent fixtures on the German cultural scene. The essayist Zafer Sebocak has stated that "our generation identifies very strongly with Germany, and we want to make this a more multicultural society. We are systematically excluded from every aspect of German political life. For the last 10 years, politicians have been talking about the 'foreigner problem,' and that has created the climate we are living through today." A Turk like the seven-year-old sister of the twenty-year-old student Ozgür Bozkurt is "stamped as an outsider, even though she speaks perfect German and feels completely at home here. People of my generation are caught between two cultures. Our parents identify with Turkish culture, but we don't. We're in the middle. We don't feel Turkish, but Germany doesn't want us."[17] Many Jews in Germany, especially those whose parents were displaced persons, share much of this ambivalence but continue to feel intensely Jewish and German.

As the number of Russian Jews bypassing Israel to settle in Germany increased in the early 1990s, so too did the sense of their difference from both "German Jews" (many of whom are of Eastern European ancestry) and "Germans." And yet it was impossible to articulate this difference officially in as direct and as seemingly unproblematic a manner as was the case with the Gypsies. No attempt was made by financial means to persuade the Russian government to repatriate Russian Jews. Here the sense of obligation or guilt toward the Jews (in the abstract) overrode the xenophobic reaction of many Germans of every political persuasion to the "masses of foreigners" felt to be overrunning the country.

By March 1993, a survey released by the Salomon Ludwig Steinheim Institute in Duisburg, an institute devoted to the study of Jews in German culture, found that those Russian Jews who had recently settled in Germany were overwhelmingly contented with their choice.[18] Only 13 percent would advise against settling in Germany. Still, at least 40 percent noted that they had been discriminated against because they were Jewish, and 29 percent observed that they lost German friends when they acknowledged their religion. The overwhelming majority, some 90 percent, felt themselves at risk from the antiforeigner and anti-Semitic acts and rhetoric of the past year. Here the heightened visibility of an identifiable minority—identifiable not only because of their Jewish identity, which has to be announced, but their appearance as "foreigners" (through language, clothes, social conventions)—reflects the complex nature of the German response to the Russian Jews.

The attitudes toward "Jews" and Israel in Germany in 1992 has been explored by an extensive opinion poll taken by the news magazine *Der Spiegel*.[19] (It was paralleled by a study of attitudes toward Germany and the Germans in Israel, as if there was no Jewish Diaspora in Germany to ask.) These figures were not very different from those of the 1988 study by the Allensbach Opinion Poll concerning West German attitudes toward the Jews.[20] The conclusion was startling, if expected: every eighth "German" held anti-Semitic attitudes. Indeed 60 percent of all "Germans" felt that anti-Semitism would remain at its present level, and 18 percent felt that it would increase. And, not surprisingly, 77 percent of "Germans" who expressed anti-Semitic feelings also expressed negative feelings about the Sinti and Roma. Almost half, 44 percent, felt that "racial purity" was vital to the Germans. These figures give the impression that the "Jewish Problem" is now perceived as part of the "foreigner problem." And yet the special status of the Jews in post-Shoah Germany (a status quite different from that of the Sinti and Roma) draws this impression into question. "Jews" and "foreigners" are overlapping but certainly not interchangeable categories.

Now, it is clear that the very dichotomy of the *Spiegel* poll rests on the assumption that the "Germans" and "Jews" being polled were mutually exclusive categories. It was assumed that the basis for the German experience of "Jewishness" lies outside the country, in Israel, and that none of the Germans were "Jewish." For if the latter were the case, it would have been a survey about Jewish attitudes in Germany toward Israelis and Israel—a very different (but potentially interesting) survey. The very category of "Jews in Germany" vanished except as the fantasy of the "Germans" about "Jews." Thus the very study that documented the attitudes of Germans toward the very idea of the Jew replicated the invisibility of the "real" Jew in Germany.

If the construction of the notion of a "German" separate from the notion of the "Jew" is important, so too is the question of who (or what) is a Jew in Germany. For the traditional and legal definition of the "Jew" as someone who belongs to the established state defined religious structure and pays taxes for its support is not sufficient. Indeed, the "religious" definition of the Jew in Germany (and recently in the United States) is undermined by those who ask whether a strictly religious definition does not exclude many individuals who desire to be understood as Jews but who wish to or must stand outside of religious authority. The nineteenth-century notion of the "German of the Mosaic Persuasion" gave way, after the Shoah, to the image of the "Jew in Germany." This latter was bound, however, to older notions of Judaism as solely a religion (in contrast to the Nazi view of Jewishness as a purely racial category). Today, secularized Jews, liberal Jews, neo-Orthodox Jews, cultural Jews, Jews whose parentage puts them beyond the pale of Orthodox religious definition, all claim the title Jew. In this case, the Jewish Diaspora in Germany has become more and more "normal," looking like the Jewish Diaspora in other Western cultures. (The unresolved debate in the United States between Reform and Orthodox Judaism about whether the lineage of the father can establish Jewish identity for the child is but one example.) And yet the special history of the Jews in Germany marks this normalization as fraught with tensions on all sides. For the negative attitude of the "Germans" toward the "Jews" is measured by the aggressivity of the anti-Semites and their actions, which purposely evoke, for all Jews in Germany, memories of the Shoah.

Throughout the 1970s and 1980s, continuous desecrations of Jewish cemeteries in West Germany marked a strong undercurrent of anti-Semitic ideology present in certain quarters.[21] Swastikas, SS slogans, and quotes from popular Nazi songs, appeared with increasing regularity in these desecrations. Remarkably, those responsible seemed always to be the young, rather than unreconstructed Nazis. In one case, in 1990, three sixteen- and seventeen-year-old high school students in western Germany were arrested after defacing a Jewish cemetery with explicit Nazi slogans.[22] In eastern Germany, similar attacks occurred. In May 1990, the grave of Rosa Luxemburg in Friedrichsfelde (Berlin) was desecrated and that of Bertolt Brecht (who was not a Jew) in the Dorotheenstädtische Friedhof was smeared with the word Pig-Jew.[23] Memorials to the Shoah in Berlin were likewise attacked over and over again after 1989.[24] In the context of the increased violence against "foreigners" and "asylum seekers," attacks on memorials at concentration camp sites such as Sachsenhausen took place throughout the fall of 1992. Synagogues and cemeteries remained targets in Germany (and elsewhere in Europe). The sense of being under siege clearly became part of the identity of Jews in the new Germany. Yet it was clearly an attack on the concrete representation of the memory of the past and not on the reality of Jewish life in contemporary Germany. Indeed, the dismissal by Steffen Heitmann, in 1993 the potential Christian Democratic candidate for the presidency of Germany, of the Shoah as simply a past historical event that should not burden the present, was greeted with loud applause from the radical right.[25] Franz Schönhuber, the head of the Republican Party, strongly supported Heitmann's position, while Ignatz Bubis, the head of the Jewish community, felt that such views "would make anti-Semitism respectable in Germany." This shift in the public rhetoric of some leaders in Germany has begun to present serious problems for what it was hoped would be a common understanding of the meaning of the Shoah in all spheres of political culture in Germany.

And yet a powerful distinction was and is made between attacks on foreigners and asylum seekers, which result in deaths, and those on the memorials to the dead—whether in cemeteries or concentration camps. Why is it that Jews in general are spared the attacks while other minorities have been subjected to intense physical abuse and insult? Indeed, at least one report that a Jew was murdered by right-wing skinheads was made in the fall of 1992, only to be quickly denied by German authorities.[26] At the same time three Turkish females (one a child born in Germany) were burned to death in the northern German town of Mölln by two right-wing skinheads. Following this attack, a great public outpouring of sentiment against neo-Nazi extremism was seen in the large cities of the new Germany. Candlelight parades (the visual antithesis of the Nazi and neo-Nazi torchlight parades) by literally millions in Berlin, Frankfurt, Munich, Dresden, and other German cities attested to the public dismay that the murders had caused among German liberals and centrists. The federal government in Bonn stepped in once it became clear that local and state authorities were either not able or were not interested in pursuing the murderers; it designated the Federal Prosecutor's office in Karlsruhe to deal with hate crimes. It was only in August 1993 that the Federal Minister for the Interior, Manfred Kanther, declared that extremists from the right, who had killed 17 people in 1992, would be prosecuted with the same vigor as terrorists on the left.[27] This placed the near 42,700 members of extreme right-wing groups (not counting the 25,000 members of the Republican Party) in the same position as the infinitesimally smaller number of left-wing radicals.

The arrest of the Mölln murderers and their subsequent trial seemed to mark a move of concern from the local to the national level. But the object of this concern soon moved from the neo-Nazi's anti-"foreigner" activity (many of the foreigners were so only because of the German *lex sanguinis* that did not recognize their birth in Germany as the basis for German or dual citizenship) to the presence of foreigners (in the form of the most recent wave of asylum seekers) in the new Germany. Thus the focus of the liberal and the conservative response came to be the relationship of "foreigners" to citizenship. The liberal argument was that non-Germans should not be forced to give up their identity as, say, Turks or Poles in order to become Germans; the conservative view was that they could not be

socially integrated into the model of the "good German citizen."
Neither the possibility of dual citizenship nor the proven acculturation of the second and third generation of Turks in Germany was
understood as an answer to these views. This issue became the lit-
mus test for the critical distance between the "German" and the
German's Other. Jews in Germany were either German citizens or,
as we shall discuss below, were considered exemplary candidates
for social integration and, thus, for citizenship.

The rhetoric of the German government by March 1993 was
that the frequency of right-wing attacks on "foreigners" had declined.
My own anxiety at the time of reunification was more than valid.[28]
But I found that even the decline from 228 attacks in January and
February of 1992 to 136 attacks during the same period a year later
did not quiet my fears that the return to normal in Germany would
mean constant right-wing violence directed against those seen or
understood as different. The increase to more than 600 acts of violence against foreigners during the month of April 1993 as compared
with 420 the year before, seemed to predict a substantial continuation of this violence. Indeed, in the final week of May 1993, a series
of related events took place in the "old" German states, the former
West Germany. In Bonn, there was a long and rancorous debate in
the *Bundestag* concerning the alteration of Article XVI of the Basic
Law, which allowed unrestricted political asylum in Germany for
all those who claim (and could prove) that they were politically persecuted in their homeland. The conservative ruling parties, the Christian Democrats and the Christian Socialists, equated the presence of
so many "foreigners" in Germany with the rise of neo-Nazi violence,
the decline of the German economy, and the anxiety about the place
of Germans in the new Germany. Supported by the right-wing of
the Social Democrats, but opposed by such splinter parties as the
Greens and the Communists as well as by many of the traditional
liberals among the Free Democrats, the limitation on the right of
asylum passed. The implication was that if we start to limit the number of foreigners, everything will get better. And the limitation was
passed even though the parliamentarians were warned repeatedly
that it will not stop the immigration of non-Germans into Germany

unless, as Gregor Gysi of the Communists stated in parliament, you have an armed border with guards willing to shoot. It will certainly not stop neo-Nazi violence. Three days later, on May 29, 1993, in Solingen, a small city about thirty miles from Bonn, neo-Nazis torched a home occupied by Turks, and five women and children between the ages of 4 and 27 were burned to death.[29] The family had lived in Germany for twenty-three years. Unlike the period following the Mölln incident, the Turkish population protested for days following the attacks, and the Turkish government demanded that the Turkish inhabitants of Germany, at least those born there, be granted dual citizenship. The response was further neo-Nazi attacks on Turkish homes and establishments in the western German cities of Hattingen and Konstanz on June 6, 1993. The general consensus in Germany and Turkey was that the approval of the limitation of the asylum laws was understood by the right-wing as support for their more violent antiforeigner position. As the *New York Times* commented: "Yet sadly, the thugs can now claim a political victory. Bonn has abandoned a generous law meant to reciprocate the foreign refuge accorded to 800,000 Germans who fled Hitler's Reich."[30] Right-wing, antiforeigner violence had become part of the political reality of the new Germany and seemed to be rewarded by the official government position.

At a memorial service for the victims, the German president, Richard von Weizsäcker, stated that "the murders in Mölln and in Solingen are not unrelated or isolated atrocities, but results of a climate created by the extreme right. When young people become fire bombers and killers, the guilt lies not with them alone, but also with all of us."[31] But does the "all of us" include the Jews in Germany, or are they too seen as at risk? They certainly did not fall into any of the categories of those bearing the brunt of the attacks, for instance, that outlined by the *New York Times*: "Germany's Turks can't vote; their tormentors can."[32] Jews in Germany can, for the most part, vote. They are neither "foreigners" nor "asylum seekers." They are not visible and yet their vulnerability is palpable. Nevertheless, von Weizsäcker's statement echoed the very concept of collective guilt for the Shoah from which official Germany was desperately trying

to disassociate itself after reunification. Indeed, the German government suggested, cajoled, and even insisted that some type of exhibi-
tion concerning post-Shoah Germany be included in the Holocaust
Memorial Museum that opened in Washington, D.C., in the spring
of 1993.

The some 2,285 attacks on "refugees, other foreigners, the
handicapped, the homeless, and Jewish institutions" during 1992,
which left seventeen people dead, altered the quality of life for Jews
in Germany.[33] Moreover, the new assumption that right-wing violence would be a permanent part of German daily life for foreigners
and asylum seekers, that is, for those who appeared to be different
on the street, shaped the response of Jews in Germany. The places
associated with them had been attacked as surrogates for them. Most
Jews did not live in isolated ghettos or work at specific types of blue
collar jobs or look "poor" or "foreign" or "dark." Yet their presence
was linked in the official mind with the provision of the Basic Law
that granted asylum, a provision instituted because of the Nazi atrocities against the Jews and the limited asylum that these Jews were
able to find. Indeed, following the Solingen murders, Shevah Weiss,
the speaker of the Keneset, the Israeli Parliament, cabled his coun-
terpart in Bonn urging her to help prevent reoccurrences of such
violence. He saw this situation as a "Jewish" problem: "Germany
has German history and, after the Holocaust, Israel has the duty to
speak out."[34]

Does not the lack of direct attacks on living Jews imply that
they are not seen in contemporary Germany? Is it not because of the
inherent invisibility of the Jews in contemporary Germany? This
invisibility is due only partially to the physical approximation of the
Jew to the non-Jew in today's Germany. Other groups are simply
more identifiable, either because of their physical characteristics or,
as in the case of the women murdered in Mölln, because they lived
in areas or buildings understood as occupied by foreigners. Is this
merely the result of this greater differentiation of Freud's "narcissism of minor differences" on the part of other groups less well integrated into the contemporary German cityscape? In any case, we
also have a historically constructed invisibility, one that has resulted

from the Shoah as a shared reality of Jews and non-Jews in Germany. Living Jews are not seen because they are not understood to be present, even while their presence is the means by which other groups are constructed.

One striking example of this phenomenon can be found in the iconography of Jewish identity in Germany. On July 19, 1992, the most representative figure of the Jewish community in Germany died. Heinz Galinski had been the official head of the Jewish community in Berlin for decades and the sitting head of the Jewish community in Germany at his death. There was a state funeral attended by the president of Germany, von Weizsäcker, and most prominent politicians. Flags flew at half-mast throughout the country. Galinski was praised and mourned as a Jew who had survived the concentration camps and had decided to remain in Germany to work at rebuilding the Jewish community. Galinski's name and his image as the "good" Jew was impressed upon every citizen.

The evening of his death, I found myself in the Berlin subway, and I began, as was my usual practice, to read my neighbor's newspaper over his shoulder (a practice that wins you as many friends in Berlin as it does in New York). What I read there was startling enough to bring me to leave the train at the next station and buy myself a copy of the *BZ*, the *Berliner Zeitung*, Berlin's best-selling tabloid.[35] For Galinski's death had made the front page in a banner headline: Heinz Galinski, followed by the age-old, German sign for death, the cross. Now it is not merely that this juxtaposition was bizarre, a cross marking the passing of the exemplary Jew, but there had been a consistent attempt in the 1920s and 1930s in Jewish reference books to replace the cross with a Jewish star, meaning that at least at one point in the history of the Jews in Germany the Christian significance of the cross was noted and responded to. Here the visible invisibility of the Jew in Germany was exemplified. Galinski, the survivor, the exemplary Jew, whose Jewishness defined him in the public sphere, memorialized as a Jew, was represented in death as a German, that is, as a Christian. However unconscious this act may have been in the German context, it signified the inability to see him as a Jew and as a German simultaneously.

The inability to see Jews as part of contemporary German culture has been the case especially in the cultural sphere, where self-identified Jews have begun to become more and more visible. Certainly, the most overt statement of this blindness about the Jews in the public sphere is to be found in the work of the avant-garde filmmaker Hans Jürgen Syberberg. In 1990 he published a monograph sketching the anti-Semitic view that the Jews had only contributed to Germany's cultural decay and destruction.[36] "Beauty in art," he wrote, "was banned [after the war] as a revenge for Auschwitz" (35). Syberberg's rhetoric is contaminated with that of the far-right wing. Thus, contemporary art "is the whorehouse of time, if it is still art," a phrase clearly echoing the Nazi view of degenerate, Jewish culture (48). And the antecedents of these artists are those Jews who left Germany because of the Nazis, Jews such as Adorno and Bloch, Marcuse and Kracauer. These were the Jews who, through their manipulation of German guilt after the Shoah, came to dominate "German" culture after the war (14). His example of this is the American television show "Holocaust," which had such a powerful impact in Germany. For him it is Americanized kitsch, produced by "merchants" (*Händler*, a Nazi code word for "Jew") (55). These Jews, however, are only a shadow presence in Germany. The real benefactor is Israel, the new "heart of Europe" (78/152). This is the new cultural axis, the axis that, according to Syberberg, dominates all of post-war culture throughout the world, just as the International Jewish Conspiracy was understood by anti-Semites from Henry Ford to Joseph Goebbels to dominate world culture in the 1920s. Syberberg's views are very much in line with the notion that the presence of the Jew is felt historically in Germany (the code word here is Auschwitz), but when contemporary anxiety about the Jews is expressed, the Jews are seen to be in the Middle East or in Hollywood. This ambivalence of location has its reflection in the very real sense of danger that confronted the Jew in modern Germany. This is a sign of the "turning inward" of the new Germany, of its "increasingly self-absorbed, intolerant and culturally hegemonistic" view of those understood as different.[37]

By the fall of 1992, a new wave of heightened awareness about being identified as Jewish, about being seen as Jewish, entered German public life. The murder of the fifty-three-year-old handicapped retiree, Karl-Hans Rohn, in Wuppertal on November 12, 1992, can serve as an indicator of this heightened tension. He was attacked, beaten, and immolated by two skinheads, and his body was then dumped across the border in the Netherlands. Rohn was not Jewish but was evidently attacked because a bartender identified him as a Jew.[38] After beating him to death, the skinheads burned his body with the cry "Jews must burn!" His death was reported in the Israeli, American, and German media as that of a Jew. This increased the anxiety of Jews in Germany about their own vulnerability. Jewish intellectuals such as the writer Ralph Giordano appeared on television and urged "Jews in Germany, following the murderous acts of right-wing radicals, to arm themselves in self-defense."[39] As a result, of course, Giordano, identified again to the German public as a Jew, received death threats. In the summer of 1993, Giordano accused federal authorities of having intentionally put off the prosecution of one of the camp guards at Theresienstadt. The federal authorities' response was to begin proceedings against him for "slander and insults."[40] There are dangers in being too visible a Jew in Germany today. But most other Jews, unremarkable in their position in German society, remain at risk only if publicly identified as Jews. Although they are invisible, they continue to feel threatened.

The high profile in contemporary German cultural life of a very small number of Jews born in the 1920s and 1930s highlights the general sense of their absence. In this context one can mention Giordano. Giordano is best known as the author of *The Bertinis*, a family novel that met with great success as a television series in 1985. He was born in Hamburg in 1923, the son of a non-Jewish Italian father and a German Jewish mother. Persecuted in the Third Reich, he became a notable journalist who, during the 1980s, turned ever more frequently to Jewish themes. He is truly a "visible" Jew. In the same general camp as Giordano is Marcel Reich-Ranicki, born in Wloclawek in Poland in 1920, raised in Berlin, cultural editor of the *Frankfurter Allgemeine Zeitung* from 1973 to 1988 and now a major media star. In his writing the question of Jewish identity in contemporary Germany has been marginal but present.[41] This generation, the generation of George Tabori and Hans Mayer, is important simply because of the overall sense of self-imposed invisibility among counterparts. And the often antagonistic response to their presence in German culture of the 1970s and 1980s reinforced the overall sense that being invisible as Jews in the arena of culture was advisable.

And yet, in contrast to the relatively low level of the official response to attacks on "foreigners" and to the official attitude that the foreigners' very presence was the sole cause of hostile acts by Germans, acts against Jews were punished. (The political response to the outbreak of xenophobia was marked by the Christian Socialists boycotting the Berlin solidarity demonstration on the eve of the anniversary of *Kristallnacht* in 1992.) Thus, in October 1989, four policemen in Eutin were sentenced to two and one-half months in jail for having celebrated Hitler's birthday with swastikas and SS runes. They dressed up in brown uniforms with swastikas and stomped on a doll with a Jewish star, cursing the doll as a "Jew-Pig, Shit-Jew, Polack Jew."[42] Even politicians, such as the far-right NPD member of the city council of Frankfurt, Erich Gutjahr, were brought before the court for publicly denying the reality of the Shoah and attacking Jews "as again exploiting the Germans."[43] Likewise, in November 1990, an officer of the German navy was dismissed from service for having denied the reality of the Shoah.[44] The state's prosecution of an "Anti-Semitic Club" and its head, the lawyer Count Adelmann zu Adelmannsfelden, indicated low state tolerance for even marginal public demonstrations of anti-Semitism.[45] In October 1991, a young worker was given a DM 1800 fine for cursing his companion and calling him a "dirty Jewish-pig who should have been gassed."[46] His companion was not Jewish. Speech acts are real acts when applied to Jews in Germany, even to individuals who are only labeled as such.

Hateful speech acts against Jews are not solely the property of the far (or mindless) right. The Greens, certainly the most socially self-aware group on the left in German politics, published a brochure in 1990 called "Violence against Women and Children." In-

cluded was an essay by Beate Bongartz, the women's rights representative of the Green Party in North Rhine-Westphalia, who labeled
Jews (defined as male) as child rapists since (according to her) they
advocate the sexual violation of three-year-old girls.[47] The response
of the party leadership was to order the brochure withdrawn quickly,
but it took two public statements before they were able to disavow
the brutal, anti-Semitic rhetoric of the author.[48] This incident con-
firms my own reading of the ideology behind a work like the popular psychologist Alice Miller's attack on Jewish infant male circumcision, in which all circumcised men are labeled child abusers.[49]
Clearly German feminism has used the crudest images of Jews in its
antipatriarchal rhetoric.[50] And yet all these comments by the left and
by the right have brought forth strong and direct condemnation.
Every action does have an equal and opposite reaction. The intense
sense of Jewish difference felt by non-Jewish Germans is mirrored
by a heightened awareness on the part of the state that such feelings
cannot be tolerated when they infringe on the rights of the Jews in
Germany.

If the German cultural community simultaneously sees and
does not see the Jews in Germany, the Jewish community outside of
Germany finds the presence of a Jewish Diaspora in Germany equally
difficult to understand. In spring 1992, I spoke at a conference in
Washington, D.C., about the resurgence of Jewish culture in
post-Wall Germany. My short comments focused on the explosion
of literary and film work by self-identified Jews (many who had
"come out of the closet" as Jews in the past few years) dealing with
the question of being Jewish in Germany and Austria. Indeed this
"third generation" after the Shoah has come more and more to deal
with the problem of "negative symbiosis" as they have come to be
considered to have a German identity, to be seen as part of the mainstream of German culture, and to be published by the major publishing houses. Yet, they are also always identified as "Jewish" writers. Many, however, deny their importance, or even their existence.
In summer 1992, an extended interview was held with four of the
leading Israeli historians of Germany and the Holocaust.[51] The con-
cluding question repeated my claim that a rebirth of Jewish culture

in Germany was taking place. It was responded to with the comment that "if such a rebirth were to take place—and I cannot imagine how it could take place—I would be neither pleased nor happy. I say this quite intuitively." This view was articulated by Dina Porat, head of the Institute for the Study of Anti-Semitism at Tel-Aviv University, who summarized the Israeli (and general Diaspora) Jewish view that "it would be incomprehensible that a new Diaspora could take form on German soil." It is also the view of the seventy-two-year-old, Berlin-born Yohanan Meroz, the son of the sexologist Max Marcuse, the nephew of the philosopher Ludwig Marcuse, and the Israeli ambassador to Bonn from 1974 to 1981.

The sense that a Jewish community exists in Germany, that it is not a community tied solely to the past, that it is a part of the complexity of the present-day Jewish Diaspora, has not yet filtered into the consciousness of Jews either in Israel or in the United States. This idea has been repressed because such a reemergence of a German Jewry—which represents not only the past, the Shoah, but also a present full of conflict and a promising future—does not fit into the pattern of the Jewish memorialization of the past. Yet a new generation of Jews exists in a new Germany. For a set of complex reasons, some of them chronological, some of them "real-political," this new generation, this complicated, new "Jewish" life, is evolving in Germany, a country that had seemed to Americans and Israelis to be a world without Jews. When I was a student in Munich in the early 1960s, all of the young Jews were planning to make *Aliyah*, to leave for Israel. Some did, but most did not. Now a younger generation of Jews, this third generation of Jews in Germany since the Shoah, has come onto the scene. They are present, not just as census statistics, but in the cultural world of the new Germany and—unlike their parents, who most often dealt with their Jewishness by underemphasizing it or reducing it to ritual practice within the *Gemeinde*—the religious community organization, they are writing or making films about being Jewish in this new Germany. Indeed, the founding in the summer of 1993 in Berlin of the first Jewish High School (*Gymnasium*) since the war was a remarkable sign of this new mix of secular and religious Jewish identity in the new Germany.[52]

This new generation of Jews in Germany, truly German Jews, grew up in Germany during the "economic miracle" of the 1960s and 1970s, at a time when the Jews were only figures in an embarrassing or haunting past, not part of a real present or a hoped-for future. Indeed, immediately before the fall of the Wall in 1989, Micha Brumlik, one of the most insightful representatives of the Jewish academic world in Germany, could write without fear of contradiction: "Jews living in the Federal Republic of Germany consider themselves as Jews in Germany and not as German Jews."[53] Since the fall of the Wall, these Jews have now met the future and, for them, it is very much like but also unlike the past. And their demands for a more complex self-representation in the cultural sphere have increased. Brumlik does capture this complexity in evoking the ongoing "abnormal normality between Jews and Germans," but the walls of the "inner ghetto" that in the past generally isolated the Jews in Germany in the cultural sphere have been breached with the same power as the Berlin Wall. The "new" Germany, now the apotheosis of everything that Jews in Germany loved and hated about Germany, has other, more visible groups onto which to project its fears. Now it is the Turks, the asylum seekers, who bear the brunt of the anger and anxiety of the reunited Germany. These groups enable Jews more than ever to "pass as Germans"—which they are by citizenship and culture—as they look and sound more like every other German than do the new foreigners. Jews no longer define difference in Germany, while difference is still defined by the image of the Jew.

There is also a new multicultural Jewish mix in Germany. Many in this third generation were themselves the children of displaced persons, people from Eastern Europe who for complicated, often personal reasons remained in Germany. Not only have large numbers of Jews come to Germany from Eastern Europe, especially from Russia in the 1980s and 1990s, but some of the major cultural figures on the Jewish cultural scene in Germany, such as Irene Dische or Jeannette Lander, are American Jewish women. The conflicts in the *Gemeinde* now seem to be between the "new" Jews—the Eastern Jews, the American Jews—and the German Jews, many of whom are themselves Eastern Jews or the children of Eastern Jews. Thus, the changes in the map of Europe since 1989 as well as the changing generations since 1945 have made Jewish life in Germany in the early 1990s a very different world from that of the 1980s. And yet there are substantial cultural and historical continuities against which many of the writers and thinkers from this new Jewish culture respond. We can now observe in detail the struggles and desires of a new version of modern Diaspora Judaism, a portrait of the reestablishment of Jewish cultural life in a culture that destroyed its Jewish community. We have had such moments in the past, as in the self-conscious reestablishment of the Jewish community in England under the Protector. But never have we had a chance in recent times to examine the reconstitution of a Diaspora Jewish community under such circumstances. The post-Shoah image of a Germany without Jews has passed. Now we are at the point of observing the way a Jewish community in all of its complexity and with a unique history reemerges from oblivion.

Jewish Writing in Its German and Jewish Contexts

Two Jewish Writers

Masochism

The visible invisibility of the Jews in Germany is not solely a German phenomenon. Rather, it is at the same time a Jewish and a German phenomenon. It places Jewish writers and thinkers in Germany in the anomalous position of figures crossing boundaries. Yet these boundaries are invisible to the majority of those who live in Germany, and this is what makes younger Jews in contemporary Germany, new Jews in a new Germany, unique. For many this conflicted identity is a quality of daily life and some have made it the material for their creative work. One must stress that Jews have been involved in German culture in an uninterrupted line from the Enlightenment to the present. Even under the Nazis, the Jewish Cultural League provided a way for Jews to imagine themselves as part of German cultural life. After the Shoah, Jews remained in the culture industry and, while often recognized as Jews, they rarely if ever brought their private and public personae together, they rarely if ever evoked the conflicts existing in their world, the world of Jews after the Shoah. There were a few rare exceptions: Jurek Becker, a survivor of the Lodz ghetto as a child, wrote about the complexities of being Jewish in the immediate post-Shoah period in the GDR in his novel *The Boxer* (1976); the major German novel by the American Jewish novelist Jeannette Lander, *The Daughters* (1976), which recounts the life of three Jewish sisters in the post-Shoah world; and, to at least a limited extent, Ralph Giordano's family novel, *The Bertinis* (1985), which, while it played primarily during the Shoah, continued the family's story into the post-Shoah era. But neither Lander nor Giordano nor Becker had the "blessing of a late birth," as Helmut Kohl described it. Giordano and Becker experienced the horrors of the Shoah firsthand, and the focus of all three was on the experienced events and their traumatic effect on the post-Shoah world.

But what of those Jews who were "blessed with a late birth," those Jews whose experience of Germany was that of a nation in defeat burdened (to one degree or another) with the memories of the Shoah (or the active repression of these memories)? Here the question of the moral authority of Jews, as a class, in post-Shoah Germany, must be addressed. For the moral authority of the survivor is above question. Primo Levi, in a detailed exchange of letters with German readers about his first book, *Survival in Auschwitz* (1947), which he published only in 1986, pointed out the impossibility of the survivor ever forgiving, that is, forgiving the living in the memory of the dead.[1] What is clear from the correspondence is the extraordinary degree of moral authority attributed to Levi as a survivor by his German correspondents—this burden was (and is) real for the survivors. The children of survivors, as has been amply shown in the ever growing literature on this topic, share in this burden of authority without having experienced the horror firsthand. Certainly their burden must parallel the sense of guilt their parents felt through the very simple act of surviving. Here one has survival at one remove—real survival without the direct experience of having been at risk.

This pariah position can give special power to those who take it. The Jewish historian at the University of the Armed Forces in Munich, Michael Wolffsohn, presents his dilemma as a question of permitted choice: "How wonderful it was to be born after the Shoah in West Germany (it was quite different in the East), how wonderful for me: Unlike our ancestors we did not have to be martyrs in order to have inherited moral power. We Jews born after the Shoah were the victors of the Holocaust. And the survivors? They received this moral credit because they survived, not because of their moral quality." Here the question of Jewish power in Germany is indeed tied to the ambiguity of the position of the Jews of Germany after the Shoah. Yet Wolffsohn rejects any pathologizing of this position: "Perhaps we should give credence to reality: Jews like to come to Germany, Jews such as Daniel Barenboim, such as the Russian Jews. Masochism? Jews like to live in Germany, such as myself. Masochism? The world record for 'mixed marriages' between Jews and non-Jews is held by German Jews. Masochism? What we need is a modicum of sensitivity on all sides."[2] Rafael Seligmann stressed the function of a specific type of masochism, the desire on the part of the German to revel in his or her sense of guilt over the Shoah, a type of "permanent sense of guilt," as one of the psychological contexts in which the "negative symbiosis" of Jews and Germans functions.[3] For Seligmann this is a mere extension of the Protestant ethic in which feeling guilty is a sign of being saved. On the other hand, masochism seems to be one quality of Jewish experience in contemporary Germany.

Masochism may well be a model to consider when looking at the writings of Jewish writers of the third generation. But it is not masochism in the psychopathological sense intended by Wolffsohn. It is not self-abnegation or self-destruction but rather employing your own sense of powerlessness as a tool to shape and control those who claim to have power over you. Here the expectations of the reader as the internalized representative of this external world of power is central to the shaping of the writer's texts. But the imagined reader is present as the supposed dominator. "You, the German audience, shape me, the Jewish writer" says the Jew as writer. Yet the author writes the text as a means of controlling the audience's real or potential power over the author. This view, espoused by Gilles Deleuze and Félix Guattari in the 1970s, is especially useful for any analysis of the writings of a "minor literature," a literature that self-consciously positions itself outside a mainstream to which it certainly belongs.[4] This writing understands itself as peripheral and yet constantly relates itself to an imagined center from which it sees itself excluded.

It is clear that Gilles Deleuze and Félix Guattari, as many of the other French commentators on the "Jewish" question during this period—for example, Jean-François Lyotard—employ a series of stereotypes of the Jew, such as the "nomadic" nature of the Jew, which stem from the "Galut" model of Jewish identity. Indeed, that Deleuze and Guattari and Lyotard focus on "German" representations of the Jews rather than on French pre-Shoah and post-Shoah discourses, is indicative of a systematic projection about difference onto another, for them, "worse" cultural sphere. And yet there is value to such an approach if one is aware of its pitfalls. Thus in Lyotard's work on Martin Heidegger and the stereotype of the Jews, for example, Lyotard regards Heidegger's refusal to speak of the Shoah as a form of the refusal to remember closely tied to the role the Jews play in the cultural world of Christianity as the ultimate object of projection.[5] Jews, caught up in such a system of representation, have but little choice: They incorporate into their sense of self the horrors projected onto them and embodied (quite literally) in their physical being; they must forget what Jews are. The body reappears as the site of an act of resistance, of remembering the validity of the Jewish experience in the Diaspora that shaped and distorted one's own comprehension of one's own body. Here the basis for the masochistic model of the relationship between the writer and a potentially or imagined aggressive culture, a culture that denies the writer any possibility of a place within it while promising such access, is an understanding of self-hatred as a response to social context. Masochism in this sense is both an internal, psychological response to the ongoing tensions of sexual identity and a social process through which this internal anxiety is projected into the world. But it is not as if this world were neutral. Indeed, these fantasies often match the hostility and danger confronting the liminal figure in the world. One of the few roles in which such a liminal figure can seemingly absolutely control the world is by generating an image of that world within the world of words. In this context, the masochistic contract, the written document that lays out the relationship between the dominant and the passive figures in the masochistic relationship, comes to be the text. For the rules that determine the text are clearly spelled out in the culture (or so they seem), and the role of the writer is equally clearly defined. Jews can therefore become writers, they can create worlds of words, they can function in a position of dependence while claiming their own control over this world. For like the true masochistic relationship, the weak, dominated partner seems to be the controlling partner. Through the act of writing it appears that the writer has captured control of the world. But this world is, of course, merely a world of words. The language of resistance to domination is taken from the world of high culture, in which value is given to the languages and discourses of the cultures in which the "exiled" Jew functions. The Jew is ever denied true participation in this high culture, for the Jew is always seen as different, as apart.

No more powerful witness to this can be found than the essays of Chaim Noll, born in 1954 to a well-established Jewish family in the German Democratic Republic. He studied mathematics in Jena and Berlin and then spent five years studying art in Berlin. In 1980 he refused the compulsory call to military service and was placed in a psychiatric clinic. In 1984 he was permitted to leave for West Berlin. He has authored a wide series of stories, novels and essays beginning with *The Leaving* (1985) and, most recently, *Night Thoughts about Germany* (1992). His contribution to the debate about the role of the Jew in post-Wall German culture centers on the question of the command of German as a cultural language. He places this, however, in a particularly Jewish context. In a remarkable autobiographical essay, he depicts how, unaware of the meaning of his Jewish ancestry, he fled into the world of the book as a child.[6] Books and their language, German, take on the quality of nurturing. He describes his mother's language as being full of "temperament and a lively springing melody" (9). Driven by his own sense of difference, his dark eyes, seen by his German neighbors as "dirty," devoured books of every description—Mann, Schiller, Shakespeare, Goethe. According to Noll, this was a way of escaping the unspoken loss in his family, the inarticulated inheritance of the Shoah in the GDR. One day he discovered Heine's letters and suddenly "understood" that this desire to flee into the world of letters was a marked "Jewish" trait. The Jews were, according to a Heine letter he quotes, the People of the Book, not the Torah, but the book as an Enlightenment icon— "a book is their fatherland, the dominator, their joy and their sorrow" (29). Heine's view of the book as the force dominating the Jew as well as giving the Jew succor projects the masochistic model back into the age of Jewish emancipation. Only later does Noll read the Bible, but he comes to understand his seeking refuge in the "book" as an articulation of his Jewishness. And, after much thought, he comes to the conclusion that being Jewish "is the toleration of other interpretations" (131). Here is the German author as Jew, who defines himself in terms of his command over a Jewish manner of using the German language, which is itself an artifact of the Enlightenment myth of universal toleration. Noll sees his writing as a new form of "minor" literature, a literature very much part of and yet separate from the mainstream in which he writes.

"Minor literature" is written in a form of discourse that must at one and the same time be employed and transcended. It is a language and style that the "minority" is accused of not being able to command. Thus the demand of high culture is that Jews adapt the discourses that mark that culture while at one and the same time they are denied access to it. In Germany, after the *Churban*, this means a highly psychologized political literature, for the creation of a "minor literature" means a struggle with the image of the self, which is in both the private confines of psyche (and thus the model of the masochist is an appropriate one), and in the public, political realm, where the resistance to the internalization of labeling oneself is always inherently political. This public and political face is articulated in the self-awareness of the "negative symbiosis" of Jews and non-Jews in contemporary Germany. But this "negative symbiosis" is inscribed in the texts generated by these writers in a wide range of responses from a desired identification to a frightening distancing from the Other. Central to the existence of such a minor literature is a clear association with the discourse about the body of the writer— bodies and biographies are never peripheral to the construction of the notion of a "minor literature." For no matter how the notion of a "negative symbiosis" is articulated, it always comes back to an inscription on the body. It is the notion that identity, the seemingly fixed summary of the internalization of a series of external norms about oneself, is rooted in both the physical sense of oneself and one's ability to recount one's biography. For the image of the collective into which the writer is forced by the hegemonic discourse of the society and literature in which the writer exists or which determines the writer's cultural orientation is always encapsulated in that society's image of the body.

The writer's tongue is but an extension of that fantasy body. Elias Canetti presented the anxiety and the dangers of the writer's tongue in his memories of childhood, where the spoken language of the Jews in Eastern Europe (for him Ladino) marked the Jew's sexuality as well as the Jew's consciousness. It is this body that is the body dominated. It is the masochist's body. It is a construct of the author (as much as the writer makes a construct of the entire fiction). The fiction of control is at the heart of the concept of a "minor literature." For in the fictive scene the writer creates the image of the dominated and the dominating using a language over which the writer is denied control. It is the enactment of this very scene of domination which places the writer (at least in the author's fantasy) in the ultimate position of control over the fictive bodies in the text. This position is analogous to the perceived position of the "minor" writer relative to the dominant culture. The writer is part of that culture, part of the contract between the dominated and the dominating, and yet separated from it as widely as the conceptual space that separates the dominated from the dominating.

Deleuze and Guattari see Franz Kafka as the exemplary masochistic author. Indeed, the very term "minor literature" is one coined by Kafka, who tried, in his diaries, to understand his own complex relationship to the "German" cultures in which he had to function as a German-speaking Jew in Prague, who related to Vienna (as a place of official culture) but also to Berlin (as a place of avant-garde culture). "Minor literature" in Kafka's world is both colonial and subaltern—it uses the cultural traditions of the world in which it finds itself as well as assuming an enforced separation from this tradition. In the literature of the "negative symbiosis" we have a turning to a postcolonial discourse. I would argue that the visible invisibility of Jews in contemporary German society replicates in many ways the situation of the Jewish, tubercular, male, German-language writer, Franz Kafka, in the Prague of his time. The difference is that the *Churban* showed how extremely tenuous identification with the aggressor can be as a means of creating identity. Kafka's awareness was part of a process of internalization of the dangers under which he seemed to exist; Jewish writers in today's Germany experience life after Kafka's dance on the volcano. Their "minor literature," like his, makes certain demands on the cultural life in which the authors function. But their ambiguity is one articulated in the works themselves, one that has become the theme of Jewish cultural life in Germany today. And it is a theme expected by the non-Jewish readership in Germany. "If you are to be visible as Jews in *our* culture," these readers demand, "then explain yourself to us. We really need to understand how you are like us but also how you experience the world differently. For you are different—you are the survivors' children; we are the murderers' children."

Without forcing the analogy, one can read the scenarios which are presented by the "minor literature" as scenarios of writers standing *within* a literary culture who belong historically and culturally to this tradition and yet who see themselves, for powerful historical and cultural reasons, placed outside or beyond this tradition. To imagine that one does *not* belong to a tradition is one thing. It enables one to stand outside of it as if an observer (like the tradition of the German writers in Paris from the eighteenth to the twentieth century, from Baron Grimm to Heinrich Heine to Walter Benjamin). To both belong and not belong, to be both visible and invisible in a culture, does demand the construction of complicated psychological structures in order to both cope with this positionality as well as to be creative (however that is defined) within the culture to which one needs to belong and feels that one can never quite belong.

Rafael Seligmann

Of the third generation of Jewish writers in post-Shoah Germany, the most radical or perhaps the most reactionary is Rafael Seligmann. Born in the British Mandate of Palestine in 1947, when he was ten he came back with his parents to Munich, where he was educated and still lives. Trained as a political scientist, Seligmann became one of the German experts on Israeli defense policy. His published dissertation drew on his linguistic expertise but also implicitly on his role as a Jew serving as the cultural interpreter of "Israel," the homeland of the Jews, and of "Germany."[7] Seligmann was a "sabra," an authentic "new" Jew, but not yet the "tough Jew" (to use Paul Breines's term) associated with Israel following the 1967 war. Yet Seligmann as an adult identifies himself neither as Israeli (read: "foreign" Jew) nor as German (read: non-Jew). Seligmann comes to understand himself not merely as a member of the Israeli Diaspora in Germany but as a German Jew. He published (as of late 1992) two novels and a detailed volume chronicling his view of the history of Jews in Germany and his own position in that history. The very sense of self-reflection in Seligmann's work leads one to want to examine his means of controlling the environment that he so intensively represents. In 1988 Seligmann, who had been a political scientist at the University of Munich, published his first novel— *Rubinstein's Auction.* It was published with a vanity press as all of the commercial houses that initially expressed interest, even excitement, about the project had strong second thoughts when they considered the image of the Jew the novel contained.

Rubinstein's Auction is a narrative of teenage *Angst* and sexual repression which fits very well into the long history of the German adolescent novel.[8] But, unlike this tradition in all of its fin-de-siècle glory, its protagonist (and his family) are Jews. And "good" Jews in literature, like Nathan the Wise, don't have sexual problems—only "bad" ones do, for instance the protagonist of Artur Dinter's proto-Nazi racist novel, *The Sin against the Blood.* These "bad" Jews, who lust after non-Jewish women, are certainly not "good" Jews. This theme represented a special problem after the Shoah in Germany with regard to Seligmann's novel, a problem not incidental to the book's shaping and reception. For the novel was already billed, in its initial publication by the Wander-Verlag, as a German *Portnoy's Complaint.* Jewish reviewers of the novel immediately picked up this theme, as did the anonymous reviewer of the first edition in the *Jüdische Zeitung,* who labeled the main character a "Munich Portnoy full of Chutzpe."[9] But the theme of Seligmann as of Philip Roth is a reflection of the intense anxiety of being seen, of being made visible in German (read: Western German) society.

Seligmann understands this theme to be internalized in the writings of many current Jewish writers, such as the Prague-born Maxim Biller and the New York-born Irene Dische. Seligmann traces their intellectual ancestry from the Jewish German satirists of the Enlightenment up to Roth and Woody Allen.[10] This Jewish tradition now has a new German continuation in the work of writers of the new generation. Roth represented for Seligmann (as well as his publisher) the successful, international voice of a Jewish writer who stood at the very center of his (American) culture and who identified himself as a Jew. The extraordinary success of Jewish American writing during the 1960s and 1970s (from Bellow to Roiphe) made it part of the cultural center of American letters. Seen from Germany (where most of these novels appeared in translation), the writing of Jewish American authors must have served as a forbidding yet tantalizing image of what a Jewish writer could (again) be in German culture. Seligmann's "Rothian" tone provides an appropriate model for becoming culturally visible as a Jew.

The official voice of the Jewish community in Munich dismissed the parallel between Seligmann (the local) and Roth (the international star). Manya Gutman, the cultural secretary of the Jewish community in Munich, where Seligmann resides, reviewed the first edition of the novel. She dismissed much of the novel as "rumor mongering" about the internal life of the Munich Jewish community. Seligmann is too visible and too "Jewish," in a negative sense. His Jewishness does not represent an authentic German Jewish experience. She continues her literary critique with a rebuttal of the notion that Seligmann is the German Philip Roth (a claim made on the jacket copy of the Wander edition of the novel). She dismisses this claim by saying that there is no true "Jewish humor" in the novel and that whatever the humor, the use of Yiddishism is aimed at a "non-Jewish readership which sees this as Jewish humor and which is seen as the primary purchaser of the novel." The novel is a form of self-hatred: "One getting the idea that [Seligmann] with this type of 'nest dirtying' wants to suck up to the non-Jewish readership, which is grateful for any sort of absolution for the years from 1933 to 1945."[11] Gutman's view is that any critical representation of Jewish life in Germany must be both self-hating and a boon to the anti-Semites. It makes the Jew very visible. This anxiety can be seen in Gutman's text, for in invoking the very concept of the "nest-dirtier" she brings the discussion of Seligmann's book into the arena of memory, of the Shoah. For "nest-dirtier," a term which came to be applied to Seligmann with ever greater regularity afterward, is the very term used by the Nazis before their accession to power for those intellectuals (primarily Jews) who spoke out against German political interests. Following his reading from the novel in February 1989 in Munich, Gutman again lashed out in print against Seligmann, who, she notes, gives the impression of speaking for *all* Jews, though he certainly does not speak for her.[12] This, in turn, led the leading Jewish bookseller in Munich, Rachel Salamander, to dismiss this "horrible" book as having "nothing to do with literature" and to refuse the Bavarian television network permission to film a reading from Seligmann's novel on the premises of her bookstore.[13]

The reception of the novel among those Jewish critics who wanted to see it as illuminating the inherent invisibility generated by the new status of Jews in Germany was exactly the opposite. Henryk M. Broder, at that time still in self-imposed exile from Germany and living in Jerusalem, praised the novel for its witty portrayal of this "late product of the much praised German Jewish symbiosis" and quoted Seligmann's line saying that "here [in Germany] nothing can be improved, the Germanys now have exactly the Jews they deserve and vice-versa."[14] The novel is, for Broder, proof of the truth of "Philip Roth's *Portnoy's Complaint* . . . [that] one knows the awful effect of Jewish mothers on the libidos of their sons." Seligmann is just visible enough for Broder and is "Jewish" in a positive, self-reflexive sense. In other words, he is just like Broder. By placing Seligmann in a role like that of Roth, the quintessential Jewish writer in America, Broder stressed the necessary oppositional role of the Jewish writer to dominant culture, whether it be national culture or the culture of the Jews. Broder's own sense of alienation from German cultural life in 1989 was clear, but he also saw himself estranged from official Jewish culture in Germany. He commented that "*Rubinstein's Auction* is the first work since 1945 by a German-Jewish author who has simply ignored the prevailing consensus: Whatever you do, don't be conspicuous! The anti-Semites would be thrilled! That is why it is a good deal closer to the reality of Jewish life in Germany than many other well-intentioned reports on this subject." But at the same time Broder evoked the alternate reading of the novel that the Jewish community feared: "Seligmann . . . is one who dirties the nest." Günther Fischer's view in the left-wing Jewish journal *Semit* was quite similar in its praise though much more limited in its audience.[15] The "exhibitionism" that Broder found a virtue was denounced a year later by Elvira Grözinger in that same Jewish left-wing periodical "a pseudo-literary peepshow."[16] Seligmann became a sign for the "crisis in [today's] Jewish-German literature." The crisis is manifested by Seligmann's sexuality, a sexuality that mirrors and represents the "exhibitionism" that Jewish writers need to show as Jews in order to claim the attention of their non-Jewish readers.

In *Nudnik,* the youth magazine of the Jewish community in Munich, there is the clear statement that Rafael Seligmann is no Philip Roth and his novel no *Portnoy's Complaint.* Yet Aron Krochmalnik also acknowledged that this novel is a "point of orientation in the search for the post-war generation [of Jews in Germany]." "Our problem today: We, as young Jews in Germany, are without any cultural roots worth mentioning, our family saga is similar to that of Jonny [the protagonist of Seligmann's novel]. This may seem depressing, but we are not the heirs of the accomplishments of prewar Jewry in Germany. Sadly, the rich roots of our parents from the Shtetl can no longer be integrated into our present life in Germany. That culture disappeared with Auschwitz. Thus Seligmann's 'journal intime' remains one of the rare descriptions of the realities of the first generation of young Jews in Germany after the war."[17] Seligmann is not just Jewish but truly *German* Jewish! Krochmalnik fits in with the official Jewish cultural norms in Munich and yet, as a younger Jew in the Federal Republic of Germany, can identify with Seligmann's claims, still only measuring those claims, however, against Philip Roth's role in American-Jewish writing and culture. His reading of the discourse of the novel, with its frequent use of Yiddishisms, is that it is not an attempt to pander to a German (non-Jewish) reading public whose notion of the modern Jewish novel is formed by a writer of Eastern European Jewish ancestry in the United States (for example, Roth), but that it is a way to portray the Eastern European ancestry of many young Jews born and now living as Jews in post-Shoah Germany. Seligmann, in commenting on this review, stresses that "his alter ego Jonathan Rubinstein does not live in the vanished ghettos of Eastern Europe nor in the Israel of Ephraim Kishon [the comic Hebrew writer who enjoys enormous popularity in Germany] and Ariel Sharon, but today, amongst us [in Germany]."[18] The Rothian world that evokes the Eastern European roots of Roth's literary tradition is now to be understood as part of contemporary Jewish culture in Germany.

Non-Jewish reviewers of the novel had quite a different response. They were almost unanimously positive in their evaluation of the novel. From rural Bavaria (where the novel was admired as "unusual and uncomfortable")[19] to Frankfurt (where the novel was admired for its "piteous gaze"),[20] the novel was praised. This was especially true in Seligmann's home town of Munich. Albert von Schirnding read it in its first incarnation in 1988 and noted that not only "was the local color exactly right" but the "sexual adventures of Jonathan reflect the psycho-social position of the generation of Jews in Germany after the war."[21] Wolfgang Görl saw the book as simply "exciting."[22] Peter Köpf reviewed the first edition in the Munich *Abendzeitung*, which also contained a long interview with Seligmann.[23] He followed this up in a long essay on Seligmann's conflicts with the Jewish community in Munich under the provocative title, "There are also Jewish Nazis." This was a quote by Seligmann from a further interview with Köpf.[24] In Düsseldorf, in Darmstadt, in Hamburg, and in Berlin, positive reviews heralded the appearance of a new Jewish voice on the German-language literary stage.[25] All of these stressed the various problems with the novel, especially its rather graphic sexual episodes, but accepted this as a valid expression of the new Jewish coming to terms with the Jewish past. But this simple validation was to be found only in the reviews by non-Jews.

In a review of Seligmann's second novel, *The Yiddish Mama* (1990), the Jewish writer Eva-Elisabeth Fischer returned to the idea that Seligmann plays the role of the "*agent provocateur* and the nest dirtier" so that he can be seen as a "critical Jew." She attacks Broder's earlier, positive review of *Rubinstein's Auction* and dismisses Rubinstein as a "mix of pornographic tirades, neurotic autobiography and subtle irony" that led Broder to compare Seligmann to Philip Roth.[26] A highly respected elder statesmen of Jewish culture in Germany (even though he resides in Israel), Schalom Ben-Chorin, in one of the newspapers published by the Jewish community, dismissed *Rubinstein's Auction* as the worst type of "nest dirtying": "If one wanted to circulate a *Stürmer* caricature of Jews and Judaism— here it has been accomplished."[27] Even in a much more positive review of *The Yiddish Mama* by Abi Pitum, this novel is seen as one in which the author had at least learned something after *Rubinstein's Auction*. What had he learned? That simple "provocation and the breaking of taboos is not enough to make an author's career."[28] Again such views are clearly in contrast to the review by the "Goyim," as Michael Zeller describes himself in his review of *The Yiddish Mama*.[29] (It is indicative of these reviews that the non-Jewish reviewers stress, through their appropriation of the type of Yiddishisms that pepper Seligmann's work, their recognition of Jewish difference.) These reviews, including one of Seligmann's reading at the Frankfurt Book Fair in 1990 and the more extensive reviews in the Frankfurt, Munich, and Hamburg newspapers as well as in the woman's magazine *Elle* and the pop-culture magazine *profil*, were all positive.[30]

All of these reviews project an image of the Jewish author as a German Philip Roth and *Rubinstein's Auction* as a new *Portnoy's Complaint*. Whether or not Seligmann consciously evoked Roth in writing his high autobiographical account of a Jewish teenager growing up in Munich, the evocation of Roth's position and the critical response to *Portnoy's Complaint* provided Seligmann with a new literary persona. A sense of the audience for Seligmann's first novel is not easily discernible from the text. One might add that Seligmann's most articulate advocate during the struggle to get his first novel published was the survivor-author Edgar Hilsenrath, whose sexually explicit and highly controversial major novel, *The Nazi and the Barber*, encountered similar problems of publication in German after its appearance in English.[31] The notable film and cultural critic Gertrud Koch simply dismissed Seligmann's first novel as a piece of naïve writing,[32] a charge that has often been leveled against Hilsenrath. With this sudden visibility within the Jewish community, Seligmann, like Roth after his condemnation by the editors of *Commentary* and in a wide range of Jewish opinion in the United States, assumed the position of the embattled Jewish writer in Germany, whose truth-telling became the stuff of his work. And his response as an author was remarkably similar.

Seligmann published a long, complex defense of his mode of writing comparable to Philip Roth's 1975 collection of essays sparked by the *Portnoy* controversy.[33] Seligmann's text combines a double focus—a history of anti-Semitism and the Jewish response that frames his account of the *Rubinstein* scandal—a scandal on a much more local level than that of *Portnoy's Complaint*. It is a complex text centering on the publication of his diary for the months following the publication of his first novel.[34] Published by the renowned liberal house of Hoffmann and Campe, it recounts, among other tales of personal literary experiences, the way Hoffmann and Campe eventually refused publication of *Rubinstein's Auction* because they were afraid that it would be taken as anti-Semitic. Seligmann's reconstruction of his experience after the model of Roth's is important as it is a claim for a triple visibility as a Jew in Germany: in the eyes of Germans, of Jews outside of Germany (read: Israel), and of Jews in Germany. Central to his undertaking is a claim to being visible as a Jewish writer, one who writes about contemporary Jewish topics for a general (read: German) audience in the new Germany.

He summarized his argument in the op-ed essay for the leading German news magazine, *Der Spiegel*, in the winter of 1992.[35] Called "Jews Live," it placed the claim of a necessary Jewish presence in Germany today in the context of a carefully reconstructed history of the Jews in Germany during the twentieth century. His charge is that the Jews must be freed now from their new "ghetto," the isolation they have imposed upon themselves by their attempt to live in Germany but not be part of German cultural life. Jews in Germany must understand themselves as German Jews, not in the romanticized sense of a German Jewish symbiosis, but through coming to terms with the immediate reality that by remaining in Germany, by having children who remain in Germany, they have acquired an obligation to articulate their "special status" as Jews in Germany after the Shoah. This obligation has been avoided by some with the claim that the Jews are *in* Germany but not *of* Germany. Seligmann charges that Germans, too, have been more comfortable with the existence of a Jewish past than with a Jewish presence in Germany. Only in the 1980s, he notes, did a new articulation of this Jewish identity in Germany begin; this still unformed Jewish identity has now come into conflict with all of the questions of German (and European) identity arising from German reunification. Older Jewish intellectuals, he says, sat back and rested on their remembered glories while writing about a lost world. He charges them (mentioning Friedrich Torberg, Hilde Spiel, Hans Weigel, and Ralph Giordano by name) with having avoided the conflicts of the present for the memories of the past. He accepts the Polish Jewish critic Marcel Reich-Ranicki's claim, which he cites, that no Jews were left in Germany after the Shoah who could document the daily struggle for Jewish identity in the new German states. He ends with a warning that the new confrontation about Jewish identity will be "shrill" but necessary to end the isolation of the Jews in post-Shoah Germany: "Jews have been a part of German society for a thousand years," he concludes, "it's about time Jews as well as non-Jews finally accept this."

The response to Seligmann's "shrill" cry for visibility as a living Jew came in a subsequent issue of *Der Spiegel*.[36] (This was certainly very different from the total lack of response that a similar editorial in a Munich newspaper evoked in 1988—shortly after the initial publication of his first novel.)[37] The answer to Seligmann was written by Ralph Giordano in a long letter documenting his own involvement in this tradition (which had more a popular, polemical twist than a strictly literary one). Remember that it was Giordano whose anxiety about his own heightened visibility as a representative Jew in Germany made him advocate that Jews carry weapons to defend themselves. Now it is Giordano who wishes to document his own presence as a Jew in this world of representations. Two more letters appear as well: one (evidently by a non-Jew) praising the essay as the "wonderful present of a Jew to us Germans," and the other from a self-identified Jew from Munich who dismisses Seligmann as an "apostate" who is demanding to set the ground rules for the way "good German Jews should act." Both these letters enact Seligmann's central thesis: The first, "philo-Semitic" letter isolates and distances the Jews in Germany, the second labels him as a "nest-dirtier." Both deny him the status he desires, that of being a speaking Jew addressing the non-Jew in an exemplary way as a part of German society. Thus, Seligmann writes books on the notion of Jewish participation in contemporary life in Germany for an audience that finds this notion either new (the Germans) or frightening (the Jews). But Seligmann in no way questions the construction of the "new" Jew. His very background, coming from Israel with an immediate identification as a "Jew" in Germany (the account of which frames the opening of his book), stresses his own sense of visibility. Indeed, the very fact that he had to learn the German of the school yard and the classroom, a language spoken in his home but not on the streets in Israel, underscores his visibility and cultural difference. He writes of the intense attraction of German Jews for their language (77) and the pain that he had to undergo to adapt to this language, the language of his parents, of the home, the language of his cultural experience. For he came to Germany able to speak German but totally unable to read or write it (14). Learning German was a significant part of his understanding of becoming one with German culture—a culture that initially saw him as an outsider, as a foreigner. Or so his account of his schooling in Munich tells us. The production of a text, whether it be a dissertation about the Israeli experience as seen from "German" eyes or a novel on the new Jewish experience in Germany seen from "within," creates a new position for Seligmann, that of the cultural insider. With this work, Seligmann is no longer, as Jack Zipes rightly commented about his novels, "tentative in writing for a German public."[38]

As of the winter of 1994, Seligmann's most recent work, a long play with the title "Good Night, Germany," was available only as a performing script from the publishing house of S. Fischer, one of the most distinguished mainline houses in Germany.[39] This work constructs a talk show in which slightly disguised soccer players, liberal theologians, political conservatives, feminists, as well as Jewish intellectuals, such as the critic Marcel Reich-Ranicki, are condemned by their own self-serving words. Central to the drama is the demand that the Holocaust cease to be the sole basis for the relationship between Germans and Jews in contemporary Germany. The central incident, the on-camera death of the critic, is based on the actual death of the Austrian American Jewish psychoanalyst and professional talk show guest Friedrich Hacker during a talk show in 1989. Seligmann adds a Rush Limbaugh-like touch with his representation of feminists and skinheads interrupting the taping and the glee of the director and moderator at the effect such events will have on their ratings. Everything has become publicity for Seligmann, even the Holocaust and its after-effects. Here, as in his autobiographical writing, Seligmann attempts to satirize the cult of the victim, whether Jew or woman (or defeated Nazi). His language remains sharp; his portraits are aimed at the German viewer, who is shown as dismissing all of the characters as having their own, private agendas in mind, not the greater sense of a new and positive German identity in which even the Jews can share.

Seligmann's texts and our reading of them provide a powerful example of the contradictions and demands involved in such a Jewish presence in contemporary German cultural life. In them, one can see the contradictory desire for visibility and the anxiety aroused by being visible in the "new" Germany. Seligmann's sense of the role that the Jewish intellectual must play in this world is tempered by his sense of vulnerability as well as by his desire to establish himself as part of this new Jewish intellectual elite, to paraphrase Jakob Wassermann, as a Jew on the street, in the bookstores, as well as in the home. Even more, he wants to use this experience of Jewish life in contemporary Germany as the focus for such public visibility.

Esther Dischereit

One can contrast Seligmann's intense demand for a Rothian literary visibility with the work of Esther Dischereit. Dischereit, born in Heppenheim in rural Germany in 1952, is the daughter of a non-Jewish father and a Jewish mother, a survivor of the Shoah, and was raised "consciously as a Lutheran, but to a decent degree."[40] Yet she was forced to deny her mother's identity: "It was clear that one could not speak publicly about this. One could not say openly: 'My mother is a Jew.' But we did not know exactly why. We saw films about the concentration camps very early, surely earlier than other children, but our mother never commented on these films. . . . Thus we learned that it wasn't 'normal' and not without risk to say: 'She is Jewish.' She also said expressly that it wasn't anybody's business. But she also didn't tell us that we were Jewish. She didn't say it. She simply left it open." After her parents divorce, she and her mother moved to Frankfurt where the "hidden secret" of her mother's identity could be articulated. There they found a Jewish community and the "anonymity" that made it possible to "become Jewish." "Being Jewish" for Dischereit meant that she began to identify herself as religiously Jewish, "celebrating the Sabbath and the High Holy Days and attending the *Gemeinde,* but not very often."

Dischereit's search for a Jewish identity after the Shoah parallels that of Jurek Becker, the survivor author, whose first novel, *Jacob the Liar* (1969), described the existential realities of life and death in the Polish ghetto. This, however, was followed by two major novels, *The Boxer* (1976), and *Bronstein's Children* (1986), whose major theme was: How does the world make Jews? This is the central question of *The Boxer.* When his son Aron, whom he rescues after they had been separated in the Shoah, decides to go to Israel and eventually dies in the 1967 war, the protagonist wonders who could have "made a Jew" out of him? "A child of Catholic parents can choose, when it comes of age, freely to remain or not to remain Catholic. Why then, he asked me, are the children of Jewish parents denied the same right?" (298). Aren't people, people, Becker asks, in an early interview.[41]

Living in the GDR in the 1960s, "being Jewish" for Becker was a free-floating signifier, unattached to any reality. For Dischereit it is attached to the notion of a religious identity, but only in the most exterior manner. Dischereit says as much in her own discussion with her daughter: "I would say today: There are human beings and Jews. Recently I went with my daughter to a country where it is inopportune to say publicly that one is a Jew. I said to her that she shouldn't speak about it. She was only five years old, and when we crossed the border in our planning, she said to me: 'That's o.k. Then I am only a human being.'" Dischereit's own personal struggle to see her self-consciously submerged Jewish identity as capable of articulation led her, after complex and difficult experiences, to create two of the most difficult and hermetic novels of post-Shoah Jewish writing in Germany.

For Dischereit the act of writing is political as well as aesthetic. Her plays, "The Red Shoes" and "I Take the Color from My Skin," reflect her intense preoccupation with the social role that Jews and women play in her Germany. The latter play, written for the radio, represents a Jewish woman abused by her non-Jewish husband, who abuses her own child in turn. The central character is completely defined by her German context, and much like Dischereit as a child, she has no Jewish milieu to help her find a positive self-definition as a Jewish woman. This is an overtly political play, reflecting on the absence of a context for a Jewish/feminine identity in Dischereit's image of Germany. In a simple retelling, it seems to be much in the line of the work by Alice Miller that we shall discuss in the final chapter. But the language, tone, and structure of these works are overt and self-consciously postmodern, reflecting on the medium in which they are presented and its limitations and advantages. Their language is intense and abstract, and the voices are clearly nonrepresentational in any mimetic sense.

Dischereit recognizes her non-Jewish audience's difficulty in identifying with her central problem—how to construct an identity

as a Jew and a woman in post-Shoah Germany. Her works themselves are as highly fragmented as she senses Jewish and female
identity to be. Her claims on a postmodern feminist politics of identity, claims made by a whole series of women writers in the Federal
Republic in the 1980s, both before and after 1989, are heightened
because of her self-conscious awareness of the complicating factor
of her self-discovered Jewishness. Her writing becomes a
self-conscious attempt to come to terms with this multiple identity.
She stated in a recent interview: "Such writing [as mine] has a touch
of prostitution—Jewish prostitution—I know, but the alternative
would be to be silent. Thus I see no other possibility except to take
this into consideration. Naturally there are other residual effects: One
must always assume that the representation of complex relation-
ships to a non-Jewish public will evoke certain anti-Semitic expectations. But there is no other way—neither censorship nor
self-censorship. I believe that writing naturally has something to do
with a *kitschy* search for truth—in any case, new truths or inner truths,
certain insights that I must take into consideration whether they
please me or not."[42] Her politics of identity are clear. She addresses
the "general" (i.e., non-Jewish) reading public in Germany as would
a Jewish writer who is aware of all of the expectations about the way
Jews are supposed to sound and represent themselves. When she
evokes the attraction of the Jewish woman for the non-Jewish man
in *Merryn*, for example, she uses all of the classic stereotypes of *la
belle juive*, the beautiful Jewess as seductress, but reverses them. In
her version of this seduction, the woman is the victim, not the young
man. Unlike the analogous play with sexuality across the boundary
existing between Jew and non-Jew in German culture that we find
in Seligmann's novels, her texts deny the reader easy access to her
voice. Their intense fragmentedness precludes that easy dialogue
between writer and reader. Thus little criticism has been lodged from
within the Jewish community concerning her "misrepresentation"
of the Jew. She is never attacked as a writer who would "dirty the
nest," but is seen rather as a complex, difficult writer.

In her experience, Dischereit thus represents a counterpoint to
Seligmann. Seligmann's secular, Jewish/Israeli identity, forged in

the early years of the state of Israel, and his feeling of displacement in the world of Germany have forged an openly expressed need to identify with it and, at the same time, an awareness of the costs of that identification. Dischereit "came out of the closet" in terms of her Jewishness. It was initially hidden rather than trumpeted. Her sense of German identity was not that of the Other, but rather, in real terms, that of an initial, superimposed identity.

Dischereit's career was also quite unlike Seligmann's. Following school, she did an apprenticeship in industry, served as a data processor and secretary for a union, and then began to work as a journalist. She was deeply involved with the left during the 1970s. In 1985, she published a children's book.[43] She was actively part of a jazz and poetry collective in Frankfurt. In 1988, shortly before the fall of the Wall, she published her first and most successful novel, *Joëmi's Table: A Jewish Story*, with the leading German publishing house, Suhrkamp. She then moved from Frankfurt to Berlin. In 1992, her second, more complex novel, *Merryn*, appeared with the same publishing house.

Both novels trace being Jewish, being a woman, and being decentered in German society as analogous problems. Dischereit comments that being Jewish in Germany is very different from being Jewish in America: "There a Jew is one who accepts the role." In Germany, she comments, no one accepts this role without struggle. This struggle is documented in the closely written novels of Esther Dischereit. If Seligmann's model is the masculine discourse of the Jewish American novel exemplified by Philip Roth, then Dischereit's text reflects the feminist voice of the best of the German feminist writing of the 1980s, specifically the narrative complexities of Christa Wolf's *Cassandra* and the avant-garde poetry of the Austrian poet Friederike Mayröcker.

Dischereit's models are clearly those from post-Shoah modernist German high culture. Her sensibilities, unlike those of Seligmann, relate to the model of a German definition of the Jew. She sees "being Jewish is something exotic in a Germany where many people have never seen a Jew." Being the exotic does not mean, however, being the object of hatred: "One does not meet open anti-Semitism here anymore." Most important, it means being in a language. In Seligmann's sense of transition, Jewish identity in Germany can be shaped by the notion of the Jewish in American culture (even if it is found in the German translations of Roth and Bellow). For Dischereit, language remains the defining moment of the cultural experience. This idea is articulated through the anxiety about exile found in the Jews in Germany in the 1950s, Jews who always kept their bags packed for a quick exit: "That is always the first question—why don't you go [to Israel], that is, where your people are? But I don't find that a possibility, and they are not under all circumstances my people. There is, for example, a political situation in Israel which makes it impossible for me simply to say: This is my country and I would feel at home there. . . . I don't have, so to say, a packed bag. I live, naturally, with the fear that I won't recognize the moment when I have to separate myself from my language. So many have missed that moment, because they couldn't or wouldn't see. Thus I have packed ideas, but no packed bags."

In *Merryn*, Dischereit stresses continuity with the Jewish past in Germany, with the inheritance of the Shoah, but she places her story in the Germany after the Wall. Suddenly, her sixteen-year-old protagonist can visit the section of Berlin where her grandparents, who were murdered in the camps, had lived:

> Prenzlauer Allee? The fall of the Wall, the collapse, the victorious factory accident that opened the gates. Reclaim property. Should she reclaim the "Jewified" apartment of her grandparents? That time has passed. The sewing room in the back, iron, chairs, table, commode, and the usual china. Value: 800 Reichsmarks, it's in the files. Infested with vermin is checked off. On the file, 10 March 43, under it the number of the deportation. The Auschwitz deportation. [77] (Translation mine.)

Jewish sensibility about the meaning of the Wall as a sign of German guilt reappears in this passage. The Wall, built in 1961, came to mean different things for Jews in Germany—especially after it became a part of their psychological as well as physical map of the city. Edgar Hilsenrath, a German Jew and survivor of the Shoah who experienced post-Shoah exile in Palestine and then in New York, returned to West Berlin (not, he stresses, to Germany) in 1975. In

1983, Hilsenrath articulated the idea that the Wall depended on the politics of the world beyond Berlin:

> Hey Mr. Tour Director! Is this Berlin?
> This is Berlin!
> And that over there?
> That is our Wall!
> Our common wall?
> Yup.
> The Berlin Wall?
> Nope.
> What is it then?
> The German-German Wall!
> But it's low!
> Appearances deceive.
> You think.
> Yup.
> How high is it?
> It's very high.
> As high as the sky?
> Even higher.
> How high?
> All the way to the horizon that marks an easing of tensions.
> The easing of tensions among the superpowers?
> Yup.
> Pretty dangerous height?
> You're right.
> Could easily collapse.
> Perhaps.
>
> Mr. Tour Director!
> Yup.
> Do you happen to know who built the Wall?
> Of course.
> Who?
> Adolf Hitler.
> Wasn't he a house painter?
> Nope.
> Was he a mason?
> Nope.
> Not a mason, a master mason?
> Nope.

What was he?
A cemetery architect.
Of course.[44]

In the fantasy of many Jews, the Wall was constructed some-how as the physical embodiment of the Nazi defilement of the city, a sort of political *Nachträglichkeitseffekt*, a trauma experienced dur-ing the 1940s which produced symptoms only in the 1960s. It is these symptoms that haunted Jewish writers in Germany after 1989. What would happen to the sense of a Jewish presence when the one living monument to the Shoah and to German guilt for the murder of the Jews, the Wall, vanished?

By November 1988, Dischereit had joined the ranks of the ca-nonical "Jewish" writers in Germany. She appeared in Frankfurt at an all-day conference called "Writing after Auschwitz" along with writers of an earlier generation such as Stefan Heym, Walter Janka, who survived in exile, and Jurek Becker.[45] There she read the open-ing sections of her recently published novel, *Joëmi's Table*, subtitled *A Jewish Story*. The reception of this complex novel shows the shift in the sensibility of readers (or at least professional critics) for diffi-cult and hermetic "Jewish" novels even before the fall of the Wall. What is perceived as particularly "Jewish" in the texts is of impor-tance in their reception.

In Ulrike Kolb's review of *Joëmi's Table* in the *TAZ*, the liberal Berlin daily, the "splintering of memory," the epiphanic style of Dischereit's texts was stressed as a positive virtue.[46] This novel, the story of a Jewish mother, Hannah, and her nameless half-Jewish daughter (referred to only as Hannah's daughter throughout the novel), is represented as a series of discoveries. The difficulty of the text is emphasized: "Esther Dischereit's language is not a normal one. It is hard to open the text, but that is its advantage. If one reads it a second or third time the splinters with which she works come together as a clear window." Dischereit herself is quoted, in an in-terview she gave Kolb before one of her readings, as saying that *Joëmi's Table* is a "sad book." It is a sad book, Kolb maintains, be-cause it shows the inherent contradictions of being Jewish in Ger-many. Kolb notes the tale of Bernadette, whose conversion to Catholicism and attempted suicide could not purge her of her Jewishness. What is striking about the passage quoted by Kolb is its stress on the femininity of the figures, for this novel is as much, if not more, a novel of feminine Jewish sensibilities in a German, patriarchal world.

Agnes Hüfner, in the leading German daily, the *Frankfurter Allgemeine Zeitung,* also underlined the "Jewish" aspect of the novel, seeing *Joëmi's Table* as a work about the "hesitant approach of an adult woman to her Jewish ancestry."[47] She places it in the context of Peter Sichrovsky's 1985 volume of interviews with young Jews in Germany, which stressed their isolation and despair. Hüfner understands that being "Jewish" for Dischereit has little if nothing to do with religious belief, rather it is a "cultural tradition" she seeks. But again the review stresses how difficult the text is: "Sometimes the prose is rhythmic, sometimes colloquial, every once in a while there are descriptions in the style of the *Roman Nouveau.* The confusion is almost perfect, rather out of clumsiness than conviction." Here the thread of Seligmann (and one might add Hilsenrath's reception) is picked up. Here we have someone writing out of a naïveté that comes from the inner conviction and experience, from the Jewishness of the author.

The complexity of Dischereit's Jewishness is stressed in Gabriele Winter's review of *Joëmi's Table.* Dischereit represents the idea of the minority in Germany: "The past captures the present. Too often is the "Jew" (this scapegoating function is interchangeable with other minorities) felt and spoken of as the Other. Only because Jews again are made into the weaker factor must Hannah's daughter decide to stand on their side, for in general she stands on the side of the weak."[48] But again the style makes the novel unique and difficult, although the complex (often confusing) syntax is felt not to be "convincing." And the fragmentariness of the volume is rooted, according to the reviewer, in the life experience of the author with her mother. The fragmentation is necessary. The inability of the mother to speak about her experiences, the review observes, has forced the author to write this book, the book of the child survivor.

Three years later, the world is very different. In the spring of 1992, Dischereit published her second novel, *Merryn*. Equally dense and complex, it recounts in fragments and diary entries the coming of age of the eponymous protagonist, a sixteen-year-old woman who, we learn in the course of the novel, is Jewish. Certainly the reception of this novel was framed by the very positive reading given to *Joëmi's Table*. It is not an "easy book," writes Beatrice Eichmann-Leutnegger in the *Neue Züricher Zeitung*, it is not "uniform" and mixes "ballad-like passages with crude language, dreams with bits of fairy tales." But this happens because the main character's daily experiences of horror and banality are reflected in the "barrenness of the topography of Merryn's world and soul."[49] What is "Jewish" in the book is dismissed in a clause: The character must go to Berlin, "where her Jewish grandparents had left few traces." Jewishness as a topic has vanished as a motivating force in the novel or in the life of the author.

Likewise, Reinhold Horn stresses the "radical hermetic" language which reminded him of the "hyperconcrete imagistic language" work of Mayröcker.[50] But it is also the language of Paul Celan's "trace of tears." Celan remains the touchstone for the writer of the Shoah in Germany. His poems, more than any other texts, define the literary response to the Shoah in German high culture. Here, even the high modern comes to be understood as "Jewish" when framed by a writer whose visibility to her audience is Jewish. This review, which does not wish to pigeonhole Dischereit as a "Jewish" writer, reverts to the easiest and most evident parallel to place her within a "Jewish" literary tradition.

On the other hand, Hanna Rheinz sees the novel as a Jewish novel, picking up on the claim, which introduces the last section of the novel, that the title character is simply rewriting the *Diary of Anne Frank*. Here the novel becomes a novel of deportation and isolation. The author's existential anxiety is seen as a reflex of her experience as a victim and her victimhood has much to do with her being misused as she is "living among Nazis today."[51] Her language is thus the "language of the inhuman, the crippled language of events, activities, and orders. It is the language of the bastard children, whose suffering remains mute, without reflection, without having been heard." Rheinz accepts the notion that Jews articulate their alienation differently because of their position in the world, or at least in terms of their position in contemporary Germany. And that position is one of bearing testimony, testimony, one might add, not to the status of the Jews in a reunited Germany, but to the long history of the Jews that teleologically ended in the Shoah. The authenticity that is ascribed to the "talking Jew," the Jew bearing testimony, is transferred to the writer seen and self-designated as Jewish in contemporary German culture. In an interview, Esther Dischereit herself stated: "When I write, I hear myself speak."[52] And this clearly happened when she read from *Merryn* in Frankfurt. This was experienced as a "unique experience" but certainly not as "beautiful." For Jews cannot be "beautiful" in their representations of their tormented world, or so go the German audience's expectations.

Unlike the initially positive review of *Joëmi's Table* in the *Frankfurter Allgemeine*, Gerhard Schulz's devastating review of *Merryn* reads this novel in an ironic mode.[53] Schulz begins by advising libraries to keep the dust jacket of the novel, for only there can one learn what the text is about. Its fragmentary nature and depiction of the central character evoke in him images of Hermann Hesse's kitschy novel of adolescence, *Steppenwolf*, and Ira Levin's potboiler, *Rosemary's Baby*. (Here the Jewish American literature evoked is from the world of mass rather than high culture.) He places it in a line of texts dealing with the language crisis which begins with Hugo von Hofmannsthal's turn of the century *Letter of Lord Chandos* and dismisses its form as banal experimentation. What he really wants from his reading of this text is explained at the end of the review. He had mentioned in the opening paragraph that the reader learns only after considerable labor that Merryn's grandparent's had been deported to a concentration camp: "This is information that one gets from the book only with great effort. Without it even the best-intentioned reader would tend to capitulate early." In the closing paragraph he notes: "Precisely today it would be interesting to take part in the experiences of a young German Jew who is looking for her place between past and present, religion and nation. As it now

lies before us, this book will only lead to the encouraging
head-nodding of some seers and the awarding of a prize for future
development. But no one will read it. . . ."

This type of hermetic text has, however, had an equally positive reception in recent German letters. When Patrick Süskind's novella *The Dove* appeared in Germany in 1987 following the world-
wide success of his novel *Perfume,* no critic recognized this as the
tale of an adult who as a child had survived the Shoah.[54] The traumatic tale of the child of deportees, who passed the place where his
parents vanished every day on his rounds through Paris, was never
seen as an encoded text dealing with the Jewish experience after the
Shoah. And the inability of this character to suffer any change in his
rigid life without totally collapsing was read as a commentary on
the general human condition rather than as a specific statement about
the same experience. Indeed, Süskind, the child of a member of the
conservative opposition to Hitler, masked this theme so well that
unlike the works of Dischereit, the novel to this day is not read in
this light. As Süskind is not a "Jew," his books are not received by
their audience as highly political comments on European post-Shoah
culture. But from the "nasal" deformities of his prizewinning novel
Perfume to the bizarre resurrection of the Wandering Jew in his most
recent book, *The Story of Mr. Summer* (1991), this theme is present.

Yet it is to Seligmann and Dischereit that reviewers go for their
authenticity. For "real Jews" are surely more qualified to tell us about
this experience than "mere" writers of any other stripe. And these
two writers, typical of the wide range of Jewish writers in contemporary Germany, both need this reading of their work as authentic
and respond to it. Neither desires to be seen as the "typical" Jewish
writer and yet both address the audience with claims that they represent a true Jewish experience. The dangers of such a claim, in terms
of the response of their readers, both Jewish and non-Jewish, is clear.
The visibility of the Jewish writer to the non-Jewish audience, however, also makes him or her "representative" of the speaking Jew in
German culture once the claim of being a "Jewish" writer has been
made. Here the Jewish reader takes umbrage. For how and why
should these writers represent the voice of the Jews in Germany,

what is their claim to authenticity? Indeed, the very claim of a German Jewish culture is drawn into question. Is there not a risk that if they are too visible they will draw attention to the Jews in Germany— and then what. . . . Serving as the "moral compass" of a nation, they say, is difficult enough. No deviancy is allowed. And visibility brings with it claims of representability.

The complexities of the new Jewish culture in Germany reflect a "real" Jewish cultural presence. "Real" in the sense that the debates, the schisms, reveal a living and breathing cultural entity. And it is virtually unique in the contemporary world. Here we have the reconstitution of a Jewish cultural identity with the self-conscious awareness of living in a country that will always bear the scar of the Shoah as a mark of the relationship between the Jewish German and the non-Jewish German. "*Noch a yohr in Afrika*" writes the South African Jewish writer Sandra Braude, "Another year in Africa? Was it possible? How long had Africa to go? Would it last? Or would it explode in a welter of bubbling passions? That was the question and no-one, no-one seemed able to give the answer."[55] *Noch a yohr in Deitschland?* Yes, for these writers, more than one year. For like Jewish writers in South Africa such as Nadine Gordimer, they too have shaped their world of culture out of the tensions of the Jewish Diaspora experience, an experience that in Germany means that their simultaneous visibility and invisibility structures their literary work and its reception.

Maxim Biller, the enfant terrible of this younger generation of Jewish writers in Germany, confronted this issue in an essay in the German magazine *Tempo* in which he describes a trip to the concentration camps in Poland while a high school student in Frankfurt.[56] This essay scandalized the Jewish community in Germany because it recorded the complex (and often inappropriate) response of young Jews going to visit the death camps in the 1980s. The theme of the essay, however, was how German Jews were forced to forget the land in which they lived. Biller's mother, who had recurring nightmares about the SS while living in Moscow and Prague, loses her dreams when she comes to Germany. Biller's own dreams about the Shoah begin only when he is in Poland. Here the act of repression is shown to be necessary in order to function as a Jew in Germany. And yet these writers write about their repression, making it visible. What does one call displaying one's own repressed emotions in order to "entertain and educate" (so the classic notion of literature) an audience that has caused the repression in the first place? Perhaps "masochism" is not the worst possible designation. For displaying one's own vulnerability in the form of a text that demands to be taken seriously as part of high culture means reestablishing control over one's identity and one's life. And such an attempt also means reestablishing control over one's body.

Representing Jewish Sexuality
The Damaged Body as the Image of the Damaged Soul

Jewish Literature in German Deals with an Old Question

There is an internalization of the complex discourse of visibility and invisibility in the works of contemporary Jewish writers in Germany. It is accompanied by the question of the nature of the body of the Jew, long a trope in the internal and external representation of the Jew. It is of little surprise, therefore, that the gendered discourse of the Jewish writer in contemporary German letters has a special status. In reading this literature, one can speak of a marking of the literary text through writers' internalization of a fantasy of their own bodies. Thus, Jewish male writers represent their difference when they inscribe their fantasies into their texts. Jews—especially Jewish males—continue to be understood in post-Shoah German society as being indelibly marked as different. For the Jewish male, because of the discourse associated with the act of circumcision and its received meaning as a sign of the covenant, this comes to define "Jewishness" in German culture. Within Western tradition, it is the Jewish ritual practice of infant male circumcision which has traditionally placed the body of the male Jew in a separate conceptual category. Jewish males were anatomically different, and this difference was represented by a clearly defined sign, the artificially altered shape of the penis. This sign came to signify the inherent difference of Jew in all matters, from the form of the Jewish body to the creativity of the Jewish spirit.[1] For Jewish women writers, the need to compensate for this double invisibility produces equally complicated literary responses.

In the early twentieth century, the internalization of the debates about circumcision, especially among the Jews of Central Europe, provided a heightened sense of their vulnerability because of their visibility. The Jew's experience of his or her own body was so deeply impacted by anti-Semitic rhetoric that even when that body met the expectations for perfection in the community in which the Jew lived, it was still experienced as flawed.[2] Such a moment is reflected in the debates about the need for circumcision among acculturated Jews in Vienna in the first half of the twentieth century. Albert Drach, in perhaps the greatest satirical representation of the meaning of the Jewish body in Austrian culture written during the late 1930s, has his Eastern European Jewish protagonist, Zwetschkenbaum, respond to the question: "What is the difference between a man and a woman?"[3] His answer, which is to be used by the court in judging Zwetschkenbaum's competency, is that "men are circumcised and women are not." For the Jew of the 1930s and 1940s, circumcision was the primary mark of male, Jewish identity. And that image is negatively charged. The extraordinary, anonymous tale of "Herr Moriz Deutschösterreicher," written in the mid-1940s, begins with an argument between the father and the mother of this "Mr. Average Austrian Jew":

> Moriz Deutschösterreicher was born on June 2, 1891 in Vienna. His mother did not want him to be circumcised: 'It's crazy, Sandor, to purposely violate my child, think about when he goes into the army and they all have to bathe naked together, or what if he marries a Christian, how embarrassing. . . . If you are dumb enough and don't have him baptized, don't do this to him. Does one have to send such a poor worm with such a handicap into the world?' She cried day and night. But it didn't help a bit. Sandor agreed with his old mother—by himself he would have perhaps hesitatingly agreed, because he did not place much store in such things.[4]

Circumcision has no positive meaning in this context, except as a means of pleasing someone of an older generation. The context of the writing by male Jews about their bodies is thus central in determining their sense of identification with the literary culture in which they live. The framing of the meaning of circumcision for male Jews in Germany during the nineteenth century provides the background to this discourse of dissatisfaction with one's own body, for it is not only the infant "Mr. Average Austrian Jew" who is to be circumcised and will grow up ill at ease with his body, but also his father, whose sense of the oddity of his own sexual body is stressed by the one person who would know it best—his wife.

After the Shoah, the meaning attributed to circumcision by Jews in Europe was that of the ultimate sign of betrayal and recognition. The Parisian Jewish psychotherapist Susann Heenen-Wolff, in her recent book of interviews with Jews who remained in Germany after 1945, uncovered the continuing power of this anxiety about the male body. Hans Radziewski, a Berlin Jew, tells her of his capture at the beginning of 1943 on the streets of Berlin.[5] He is asked how he was recognized: "Well, you had to tell your name. They asked about the [Yellow] Jewish Star, and if everything else failed, one had to drop one's pants." When he is asked how the Germans could tell a Jew from a Muslim, he remarked that because of their Arab specialists, the SS could tell whether the cut was made on the eighth or the twenty-eighth day. The powerful fantasy about the immediate visibility of the Jewish body was shaped by the sense that the body was indeed inherently different. And the marker of circumcision still remains a powerful sign of identity for Jews in Germany. In her interview with Rolf K., born in 1932, whose criminal activities in postwar West Germany led him to spend extended periods in prison, she asks about whether his son feels himself to be Jewish. The answer is no. The child's mother is not Jewish. And yet, he notes, he is circumcised—and not for medical reasons. "No, no, he is circumcised because I wanted it. And at his age he couldn't refuse. He was seven days old" (112). In contemporary Central Europe, Jewish anxiety about the meaning of the Jewish body after the Shoah becomes part of the definition of the gender role ascribed to the male Jew as circumciser and circumcised.

The Meaning of Circumcision

The very core of the definition of the Jew for medical science during the latter half of the nineteenth century is also the most salient popular factor in defining the body of the Jew—it is the practice of infant male circumcision. "In the folk-mind scarcely anything was more important than circumcision. Circumcision *made* the Jew," as the American historian Jacob R. Marcus has cogently observed.[6] In terms of the late nineteenth century, the anthropologist Richard Andree noted that in "Yiddish the very term 'to make into a Jew' (*jüdischen*) means to circumcise."[7] Thus, the male Jewish body is the base line for the definition of the Jew. Circumcision marked the Jewish body as unequal to that of the Aryan and the male Jew as the exemplary Jew. What would circumcision have meant to a Jewish scientist who had internalized the negative associations? As the anti-Semite Ezra Pound once remarked to his friend Charles Olsen: "There was a Jew, in London, Obermeyer, a doctor . . . of the endocrines, and I used to ask him what is the effect of circumcision. That's the question that gets them sore . . . that sends them right up the pole. Try it, don't take my word, try it. . . . It must do something, after all these years and years, where the most sensitive nerves in the body are, rubbing them off, over and over again."[8] The rub was a social as well as a scientific rub, as we shall see.

The centrality of the act of circumcision in defining what a Jew is makes the very term "Jew" come to mean the male Jew in the nineteenth century. Thus, we have an immediate dichotomy—all Jews, male and female, are different from the "neutral" scientific observer (who is male and Aryan in his ideology). Male Jews are uncanny, however, in that they superficially appear to be males but are not because of the altered form of the genitalia. (Jewish women are different too. They are different—different in a manner other than women are different from men, but different from the Aryan male observer.) The anti-Semitic British explorer and author, Richard Burton, commented that "Christendom practically holds circumcision in horror."[9] The perspective of this supposedly neutral observer becomes one with the space of scientific observation. The male, Aryan scientific gaze becomes the means of defining the healthy perspective. Jewish scientists, their bodies marked by the act of circumcision, cannot share in this sense of community.

It is not that the circumcised penis was in itself the most unusual biological feature of the anthropological image of the male Jew in nineteenth-century science—indeed the debates about the specificity of all of the physiological and psychological markers of difference invented by eighteenth- and nineteenth-century ethnology—from skull capacity, size, and shape (cephalic index) to skin and hair color—were employed to document the difference of the Jews from all other races.[10] But it was in the arena of this specific ritual practice that the pathological nature of the Jews was seen to manifest itself most clearly. The *brit milah,* the practice of infant male circumcision, became, for the thinkers of the late nineteenth century, the major sign of Jewish difference.[11] And all of the controversies over circumcision in medical literature were colored by its centrality as the means of distinguishing between the healthy and the diseased, between the Aryan and the Jew. As an anonymous author stated in the leading German pediatric journal in 1872: "The circumcision of Jewish children has been widely discussed in the medical press as is warranted by topics of such importance. But it is usually discussed without the necessary attention to details and the neutrality that it deserves. Indeed, it has not been free of fanatic anti-Semitism."[12] This association continues strongly even as circumcision becomes widely practiced (in such countries as the United States and Great Britain). Indeed, as late as 1920, one can read in the *British Medical Journal* the following comment on circumcision: "This injurious procedure, like that of keeping women in bed after childbirth, we owe to the Jews, and we have nothing to thank them for as regards these two of their religious rituals."[13] One might add that there is a constant strain of blaming the Jews for the dangers perceived as inherent in this procedure and present in most anticircumcision literature to this day.[14] Circumcision marks the Jew as both damaged and potentially damaging. In German popular culture of the 1980s, the sign of circumcision marked the group fantasy about the hidden nature of the male Jew's body, even when the body in question was uncircumcised.[15] And for German Jews, the internalization of the sense of their body's difference cannot be underestimated.[16]

The social significance of reliance on circumcision as the marker of Jewish difference in European medicine of the late nineteenth century lies in the overt fact that by that time, Western European Jews had become indistinguishable from other Western Europeans in matters of language, dress, occupation, location of their dwellings, and the cut of their hair. Even so, the body of the male Jew was marked as different. The debates about the meaning of circumcision in the nineteenth century must be understood in the context of this specifically European recognition of circumcision as the most evident sign of the racial difference of the Jew.[17]

But to say that it was assumed that Jews bore the stigmata of circumcision as a sign of difference is much too vague. It is clear that a wide range of meanings has been associated with the act of circumcision in the West. Circumcision has been read as a sign of everything, from sexual hygiene, to cosmetic appearance, to tribal identity or a mark of adulthood, to either diminishing or enhancing sexual desire, to increased or decreased fertility, to patriarchal subjugation, to enhanced purity, to the improvement of sexual endurance, to a form of attenuated castration, to menstrual envy, to a substitute for human sacrifice. But there are four "traditional" views of the "meaning" of circumcision in connection with the Jews which have dominated Western thought since the rise of Christianity.[18] Following the writings of Paul, the first saw circumcision as inherently symbolic and, therefore, no longer valid after the rise of Christianity. This view was espoused by the Church Fathers, Eusebius and Origen, and it continued through the Renaissance (Erasmus) and the Reformation (Luther). It forms the theological basis for the distinction which Christians were able to make between their bodies and the bodies of the Jews.[19]

The second meaning saw circumcision as a sign of a political or group identity. The rhetoric in which the accepted science of the late nineteenth century clothed its rejection of circumcision is of importance. It was intense and virulent, as has been noted, and never free from negative value judgments. One central example should suf-

fice. Paolo Mantegazza (1831-1901) was one of the standard "ethno-
logical" sources for the late nineteenth century on the nature of human sexuality. The controversial centerpiece of Mantegazza's work
is his trilogy on love and sex: *Physiology of Love* (1872), *Hygiene of
Love* (1877), and *On Human Love* (1885).[20] Cited widely by sexolo-
gists from Cesare Lombroso, Richard Krafft-Ebing, Havelock Ellis,
and Iwan Bloch to Magnus Hirschfeld, Mantegazza remained one
of the accessible, "popular" sources for "scientific" knowledge (and
misinformation) for the educated public at the turn of the century.[21]
One of a group of physician-anthropologists (such as Cesare
Lombroso), Mantegazza had pioneered the introduction of the study
(and enjoyment) of *Erthroxylon coca* and its derivative, cocaine, in
the late 1850s. Following the publication of Darwin's *Descent of Man*,
Mantegazza became one of Darwin's most avid correspondents (and
sources), supplying Darwin with a series of "anthropological" pho-
tographs which Darwin used for his later work.

If we turn to the chapter in Mantegazza's study of the anthropology of sexual practices which follows the one on "perversions,"
we come to a detailed discussion of the "mutilation of the genitals,"
which recounts the history of these practices among "savage tribes"
including the Jews.[22] Indeed, it is only in Mantegazza's discussion of
the Jews that the text turns from a titillating account of "unnatural
practices" to a polemic (echoing Spinoza's often cited comments on
the centrality of circumcision for the definition of the Jew[23]) against
the perverse practices of those people who are out of their correct
"space" and "time"—the Jews:

> Circumcision is a shame and an infamy; and I, who am not in the
> least anti-Semitic, who indeed have much esteem for the Israel-
> ites, I who demand of no living soul a profession of religious faith,
> insisting only upon the brotherhood of soap and water and of
> honesty, I shout and shall continue to shout at the Hebrews, until
> my last breath: Cease mutilating yourselves: cease imprinting
> upon your flesh an odious brand to distinguish you from other
> men; until you do this, you cannot pretend to be our equal. As it
> is, you, of your own accord, with the branding iron, from the first
> days of your lives, proceed to proclaim yourselves a race apart,
> one that cannot, and does not care to, mix with ours.[24]

This was not his view alone. Edward Westermarck, the creator of the sociology of marriage, labeled circumcision simply "the mutilation of the sexual organ."[25]

Mantegazza introduces his discussion of the sexual exclusivity of the Jews with the following passage:

> It is altogether likely that the most important reason which has led men of various ages and of varying civilizations to adopt the custom of cutting off the prepuce has been that it was felt to be necessary to imprint upon the human body a clear and indelible sign which would serve to distinguish one people from another and, by putting a seal of consecration upon nationality, would tend to impede the mixture of races. A woman, before accepting the embraces of a man, must first make sure, with her eyes and with her hands, as to whether he was of the circumcised or the uncircumcised; nor would she be able to find any excuse for mingling her own blood-stream with that of the foreigner. It had, however, not occurred to the legislator that this same indelible characteristic would inspire in the woman a curiosity to see and to handle men of a different sort.[26]

The seduction of the Jewish woman by the Other—here the non-Jew—is the result of the "seeing" of the difference in the form of the genitalia. The need to "see" and "touch" the Other is the fault of the circumcised (male) Jew, whose very physical form tempts the female to explore the Other. Here we have another form of the displacement of the act of touching (sexual contact) with the permitted (indeed, necessary) act of seeing, but with a pathological interpretation.

Mantegazza notes that "the hygienic value of circumcision has been exaggerated by the historians of Judaism. It is true enough that the circumcised are a little less disposed to masturbation and to venereal infection; but every day, we do have Jewish masturbators and Jewish syphilitics. Circumcision is a mark of racial distinction; . . . it is a sanguinary protest against universal brotherhood; and if it be true that Christ was circumcised, it is likewise true that he protested on the cross against any symbol which would tend to part men asunder."[27] This view is clearly antithetical to the view of scholars such as the sociologist Edward Westermarck and the sexologist Auguste

Forel, who link "the intention of exciting the sexual appetite" through circumcision with "the hygienic advantage of circumcision [which] took a part in its transformation into a rite."[28] "We may go to Moses for instruction in some of the best methods in hygiene," according to William Osler in 1914, even though the Jew is less adept in the world of "intellect and science."[29] The traditional view was echoed in Ernest Crawley's study of marriage, where he reported that the "Jews considered circumcision as a 'cleansing.'"[30] Mantegazza's rhetoric sets the Jew apart and makes the Jew's body a mark of his pariahdom. Jews are seen throughout Europe as "the circumcised pariah," according to the French historian Anatole Leroy-Beaulieu.[31] And that pariahdom reflects the "essential" character of the Jew, for Jewish male character has been seen as marked by the circumcised body. Indeed, in 1891 one could read the following toilet graffiti in Vienna: "You without a foreskin / shouldn't be too pushy" ("Ihr ohne Vorhaut / Seid nicht vorlaut").[32]

The third reading of circumcision saw it as a remnant of the early Jewish idol or phallus worship. Thus J. H. F. Autenrieth saw circumcision as but a primitive act practiced by culturally inferior peoples such as Jews and African blacks. Autenrieth, by 1829 the chancellor of the University of Tübingen, entered the discussion of the meaning of circumcision with a public lecture on its history. For him, as for others, circumcision was a surrogate for human sacrifice.[33] John Lubbock saw the rite of sacrifice as a "stage through which, in any natural process of development, religion must pass."[34] But the Jews also sacrificed their animals at the Temple as "symbols of human sacrifice . . . [which] were at one time habitual among the Jews."[35] Circumcision was seen as a sign of the "inherent barbarism of this people," a view seconded by a Dr. Hacker in a medical journal in 1843.[36] Here again the medical discussion of a social practice becomes contaminated by the racial context into which it is placed. Indeed, into the late nineteenth and early twentieth centuries, this view dominates the discussion of the ethnopsychologists about the meaning of circumcision as a semantic sign. The experimentalist Wilhelm Wundt says that circumcision is "of the nature of sacrifice. Along with the offering of hair in the cult of the dead and with the pouring out of blood in connection with deity worship, it belongs to that form of sacrifice in which the sacrificial object gains its unique value by virtue of its being the vehicle of the soul. Thus, the object of sacrifice, in the case of circumcision, may perhaps be interpreted as a substitute for such internal organs as the kidneys or testicles, which are particularly prized as vehicles of the soul but which can either not be offered at all, on the part of the living, or whose sacrifice involves serious difficulties."[37] For Wundt, politically a liberal in his time, Judaism is "but one of those vanquished cults which struggled for supremacy in the pre-Constantinian period of the Roman World Empire."[38] And the practice of this substitute for ritual sacrifice is a sign of the barbarism and marginality of the Jew.

The fourth reading of circumcision saw it as a form of medical prophylaxis. This seems to be claimed for the first time in the writing of Philo, who wrote in a strongly Hellenistic culture that found any mutilation of the body abhorrent.[39] Circumcision was a prophylaxis against diseases of the penis but also promoted the well-being of the individual and assured fertility. Later the hygienic rationale was also evoked, as we have seen, in the work of Johann David Michaelis, the central German commentator on this practice in the eighteenth century. Only in the middle of the nineteenth century does the debate about the medical meaning of circumcision impact upon the Jewish community in Central Europe. Prior to this time, the discussions concerning the meaning of circumcision in the Christian community remained separate from Jewish concern in Europe. While the image of the circumcised Jew was raised as a central metaphor for Jewish difference in Great Britain with the presentation of the Jewish Naturalization Act in 1753,[40] it becomes of importance only with the gradual acculturation of the Jews in Germany and Austria toward the middle of the nineteenth century. The debates within and without the Jewish communities concerning the nature and implications of circumcision surfaced in Germany during the 1840s. German Jews had become acculturated to German middle-class values and had come to question the quasi-sacramental requirement of circumcision as a prerequisite of their Jewish identity.

On July 15, 1843, a position paper by the "Friends of Reform" was published in the *Frankfurter Journal* in which the platform for a new, "reformed" Judaism was put forth. The abolition of circumcision was one of the keystones of that program. Led by the radical reform rabbi Samuel Holdheim, it responded not only to a Christian (both Catholic and Protestant) tradition that denigrated circumcision as a sign of inferiority, but also to the growing charge that it was an "unhealthy" practice.[41] Holdheim held that circumcision was a ritual that was not binding upon Jews, any more than were the Rabbinic laws concerning the observation of many other rituals.[42] Holdheim sees circumcision as having a purely religious function and as a sign of membership in the community. The sign of the covenant was understood symbolically and internally rather than as incised upon the body. He did not see it as a necessity any more than the sacrifice of the paschal lamb, a practice that was abandoned with the destruction of the Temple. Holdheim's position was the most radical in the Jewish community of his day. While he did not raise a medical objection to circumcision, such objections were already quite vocal in Germany.

In 1844 a Berlin physician, J. Bergson, a Jewish advocate of circumcision, responded to Holdheim's call for the abolition of infant male circumcision by advocating medical reforms to make the procedure safe.[43] He shifted the debate from an emphasis on religious necessity to circumcision's medical implications. As early as 1825, a Dr. Wolfers, who was a physician and "male midwife" from Lemförde, had argued that circumcision was a dangerous procedure and should be placed under the supervision of the "medical police."[44] He discussed the poor preparation of the ritual circumcisers, the *mohelim*, and the destructive results of their incompetence. Beginning in 1819, the Berlin Jewish community had insisted on a medical presence at the *bris* (ritual circumcision).[45] Danger of infection remained a concern well into mid-century. A Dr. Klein in Ratibor suggested in 1853 that such public health control was in no way a violation of freedom of religious practice but solely a question of public health.[46] This view led to one of the leading proposals that formed the background to Holdheim's suggestion: If the procedure is dangerous, then it must be abolished. The political implications of abolition were not clear to Holdheim, for in Prussian and Austrian state law, at least, if a child was not circumcised, he had to be baptized. Indeed, in a case in Brunswick in 1847, the parents, after refusing to have their child circumcised for medical reasons, were ordered to have him either circumcised or baptized within fourteen days.[47] Here the echo of the discussion of the heritability of the act of circumcision comes into play. Can Jews truly abandon circumcision as a sign of their religious identity? Or is that as useless as trying to abandon their racial identity? Given the marginal status of baptized Jews within German culture, the choice between circumcision or baptism meant, in practice, remaining a Jew, baptized or not. The inner sign of circumcision remains and can be spontaneously written upon the body through the somatic inheritance of acquired characteristics.

The Meaning of the Jewish Body Internalized in the Writing of Jewish Women after the Shoah

The implications of circumcision as a sign of the Jewish body seem to be missing in much of the writing by contemporary female Jewish writers in German such as Lea Fleischmann or Barbara Honigmann, whose works reflect on many of the same conflicts of identity as those found in the writings of their male counterparts.[48] In much of the self-consciously feminist writing by Jewish women in Germany, however, this sense of difference of the Jew's body is shared with the Jewish male, but only on a metaphoric level. In these texts, an awareness of this difference is linked to a symbolic representation, usually through the evocation of the Star of David and its historical function as the Nazi marker of the Jewish body. Esther Dischereit, for example, presents an aspect of the gendered distinction between the writing of a self-labeled Jewish woman in German culture and that of a Jewish masculine sensibility. In *Joëmi's Table* (1988), which is, after all, a novel about survival and identity formation in pre- and postwar Germany, she evokes a string of associations about being Jewish, in particular when seeing the Jewish cemetery at Fez with its new graves: "Where death is, there is also mumbling, kaddish, Passover, and circumcision. In my Frankfurt—there is no death."[49] There is no death, for all have already died and died without the ceremony of remembrance. Circumcision is central to her definition of being a Jew. There seems to be no pejorative association at all. Yet she images her own body, the body of the Jew, as inscribed with the "inherited mark of Cain, forgotten under the water of Socialism, [which] shimmers through onto [her] skin" (9). This mark of Cain (historically a common association with circumcision) is represented by Dischereit in a very different way than through the circumcised body of the male Jew. She fantasizes about her own body being transparent as she crosses the German border: "But if they demand that I should disrobe—why should they demand that— if they demand that I should disrobe, I would undress. And one would see the star through the clothes—one does not see it—through the clothes, burnt into my skin—it is not burnt, I wasn't ever there— burnt into my skin, and the dogs would come to me" (35). The Nazi's "Jewish Star" is inscribed on her sense of her own body—it is burnt into her living soul since she survived the actual burning of the body in the camps. Here the internalization of the mark upon the body, the mark of Cain usually associated with the act of male circumcision, is replaced with a metaphor of Jewish difference. But the context remains the same—it is the act of disrobing, of revealing the body which reveals the nature of the Jew. This theme is reflected in the powerful film *Hitlerjunge Salomon* (1991, released in English as *Europa, Europa*) in which the circumcised body of the Jewish protagonist can never be revealed, since it would betray him to the Nazis among whom he is hiding. The Polish Jewish director, Agnieszka Holland, struggles with the theme taken from the real life experiences of Solomon Perel, a survivor of the Shoah.[50] Unlike Dischereit, she refuses to allow the theme to become solely a metaphor. Holland reflects what Dischereit has internalized. But her image is bound by respect for the life experiences of a Jewish male in Germany seen through the lens of a Polish Jewish woman director.

An interesting problem in the discussion of the representation of the Jewish male body in German culture can be found in the work of three American women writers who confront the Jewish question in Germany in very different ways, each framing the problem of a male Jewish voice in a radically different manner. Irene Dische, raised a Catholic but of German Jewish ancestry, moved to Germany from the United States in the 1980s. Her short stories (first available in German translation) present the body of the Jewish male as unremarkable. Her major short story, "A Jewess for Charles Allen," in which an American Catholic man of Jewish ancestry rapes a German woman who claims to be Jewish yet is revealed to have Nazi parents, does not represent the body of the Jewish male as different.[51] Coming from a society in which circumcision is ubiquitous (if not universal) and from a cultural-religious background in which it does not play a defining role, Dische is impervious to any sense of the difference of the male Jew's body. Her Jewish male (who by his religious education is a Catholic) seems to possess no identifiable physical characteristics, while her Jewish female (who is in reality a non-Jewish German) publicly represents her Jewish identity by the "silver Star of David" she wears about her neck (13). Our reading of her dark physiognomy is immediately shaped by this article of jewelry—as is the reading of her by the male protagonist. She becomes for him (and for us) the essential Jewish female. The symbolic representation of the Jew's body is represented by the presence of the Star of David. In Dische's account, the protagonist is shown to be merely a repressed male, repressed in his identity as well as his sexuality, who lashes out at his female tormentor the only way he knows how— through sexual assault. Dische's own evocation of the anti-Semitic trope of the Jewish male desiring to possess the body of the non-Jewish woman, which underlies this masquerade of identities, provides a model for her understanding of the Jewish male and his sexuality. For in the end it is the Jewish male (whose circumcised state is implied though never stated) who rapes the German female. The power of the trope transcends all of the masquerades in this novel. The "Jewish Star" now marks the body of the female victim of the male Jew's anger and lust.

Dische's work is paralleled in an autobiographical vein by Jane E. Gilbert. Born in the United States of Eastern European Jewish parents, she immigrated in the 1970s to the Federal Republic of Germany, where she took up German citizenship and where she still resides. Her experiences in learning to deal with Germans as individuals rather than as a stereotyped collective form the theme of her autobiography. In this autobiography, however, there is a striking moment when she seems to characterize the anti-Zionist feelings that came to replace overt anti-Semitism among the members of the German left during the 1970s. She tells the story of a Jewish male friend of hers who meets a young German woman at a bar and goes home with her. She flees, according to Gilbert, when she spies his Star of David pendant as he undresses for bed, cursing him as a Zionist. Here the pendant (echoing the Nazi's use of the "Jewish Star" as a marker of the Jew) overtly replaces the circumcised penis, which is the most evident sign of the Jew to be seen when the Jewish male undresses.[52] Whether this is the result of the self-censorship of the author or her acquaintance is not at all clear. But the Star of David comes, as it does in the work of Dische and Dischereit, to represent the idea of difference present in the body of the Jew—as understood in a symbolic mode in German culture. That Gilbert is aware of the significance of the act of circumcision in Germany is evident from her text. An earlier anecdote reveals that a male friend of hers exposed a petty criminal posing as a Jew in Berlin through the "fact" that he was uncircumcised (176). In this context, circumcision is the mark of authenticity. In the anecdote about the conflation of "Jew" and "Israeli," Gilbert does not make the evident connection. She is appalled that these two categories are conflated. They meet in the image of the body of the male Jew, whose circumcision signifies his inherent difference from the German.

Radically different is the representation of the Jewish male body in the autobiographical work by Susan Nieman. An American of Eastern European Jewish ancestry, she went to Berlin in the mid-1980s as a student. Today she lives with her husband and children in New Haven, where she teaches philosophy. She becomes a critical commentator as well as a participant in the daily life of the city. It is there that she develops a sense of what being Jewish in Germany meant—at least for her. One of her non-Jewish lovers shocked her

by commenting that "'Every time I see you I think of Dachau . . .
baby.'"[53] But the uncircumcised bodies of the non-Jewish lovers do
not seem remarkable to her. When she finally meets Michael, the
man she is to marry, she discovers that he has a Jewish mother (but
that his father was a member of the *Wehrmacht*). But even with
Michael, there is no comment on the nature of the adult male's body.
This question arises only with her representation of the body of the
Jewish male child. When the child of a Jewish couple Nieman knows
is put into day care the question of the child's circumcision becomes
central to Nieman's representation of his difference: "'Have they ever
asked why he's circumcised?' asked Jesse one night. 'I know,' Sarah
answered. 'It really stands out when the kids are naked. No. They
haven't.' 'Afraid to ask.' 'I don't think it occurs to them'" (190). While
this sign marks the inherent difference of the Jew, it is internalized
by his parents, who note it and suppress its implications. The
non-Jewish day care workers understand that the child is "really"
different from the other children. When Susan's and Michael's child,
Benjamin, is circumcised, the description of the *brit milah* is one of
the most ironic yet moving chapters of her memoir (209–13). The act
of circumcision comes to represent the revitalization of Jewish life in
Germany. Jacob Taubes, the late and lamented professor of philosophy at the Free University (Berlin), serves as the child's godfather
and the event serves as a microcosm of the tensions in the new and
growing Jewish community—a community that now shows its fis-
sures as a sign of health. Nieman, unlike Dische, understands the
difference the Germans attribute to the marking of the Jewish body.
For her, the ritual importance of the covenant for her own child is to
no little degree determined by her sense of her own difference in
German society. Her memoir chronicles her becoming aware of her
own Jewish identity through exposure to the constant repression of
the meaning of Jewish identity in German culture during the 1980s.
The omnipresent sense of foreboding that this active forgetting created in her heightened her sense of her own identity as a Jew.

  The circumcised adult Jew is thus mostly missing from the
world of these Jewish women. This absence is a sign of the extraordinary complexity of meaning associated with the image of the cir-

cumcised male for Jewish women. For non-Jewish women, even placed in a different cultural context, this association seems to be equally complicated. The director and author Doris Dörrie, in her story "Straight to the Heart," recounts the kidnapping of a Turkish baby by a young German woman desperate for a child. Renaming the baby "Jan" from "Kenan" she brings him home to her husband, who believes the child to be theirs.

> He wanted to change Jan's diaper. Anna had to show him how. Thrilled, Armin felt Jan's arms and legs, the feet, the size of his thumb, the plump belly with its umbilical knot. Good heavens, could it be Kenan had been circumcised. . . . She noticed how her face was twitching. She would have liked to shove Armin aside. It was her baby. Hers alone.[54]

She is acutely aware that the baby's body would be marked by the sign of its difference, revealing it to be not her own. The very concept that circumcision reveals difference is made real here in the text. This sense of difference is played out to no little degree in her representation of the meaning and complexity of the male body as different to the world. But here an added aspect is introduced—the marked male body reveals difference from the self.

The Meaning of the Jewish Body Internalized in the Writing of Jewish Men after the Shoah

Recent German prose by a new generation of male Jewish writers reflects on this question of the meaning of circumcision. These texts represent a new Jewish literary sensibility in German culture in the continuing debate about circumcision begun by St. Paul. A definite division exists, however, between those writers who identify with the older generation of Jewish writers in Germany, insecure about their existence and their bodies, and those of the newest generation, whose physical difference becomes a means of setting themselves apart from the Germans (and from the "foreigners," even circumcised male foreigners such as the Turks).

It is the experience of this newest generation, which is the focus of Rafael Seligmann's "scandalous" novel *Rubinstein's Auction* (first published in 1988), as noted in the previous chapter.[55] Set in the late 1960s in the Federal Republic of Germany, the novel seems only to document the coming-to-consciousness of a young Jewish male. It presents the complexities of dealing with an identity formed by the history of the Shoah but without any personal memory or experience of these events. Seligmann's text is masochistic in that it presents, for a general German readership and in the written form of the novel, a contract—"Here," it says, "I will tell you all about how complex and difficult it is to be a Jew in today's Germany, a country that murdered millions of Jews. You will recognize me then as a writer recording an authentic experience that you cannot have but that you desire to have. For you identify not with the murderers (I hope) but with the victims." Seligmann thus needs to establish that he is *just* like every other writer in contemporary German culture (in order to be part of the literary mainstream) and completely different from every other (non-Jewish) writer in contemporary German culture (in order to offer the frisson of difference). And the locus for this visible invisibility is the male body.

Central to Seligmann's project (and to all of these texts by male Jewish writers that we shall discuss in this chapter) is the question of male sexuality and the representation of the male Jewish body as different. Seligmann's novel is indeed a tale of adolescence, adolescent rebellion, and the discovery of the sexual. But even more importantly, the novel focuses on the perceived or real difference of the Jewish body and the internalization of that difference in the structuring of the male protagonist's sense of insecurity. The alienation experienced by the adolescent male as represented in modern fiction by, for example, J. D. Salinger's Holden Caulfield, is heightened by the sense of insecurity felt by those males understood to be Jewish in German post-Shoah culture. This and other similar texts come to be as much about the meaning of the Jewish body as about any other single question. The body of the Jew, with all of its implications, itself becomes an icon for the perceived and internalized difference of the sexuality of the Jewish male.

Rubinstein's Auction begins with the incident that gives the novel its name. The eponymous protagonist Jonathan Rubinstein, in his final year in high school, is asked by his attractive Aryan teacher, Ms. Taucher, to sit next to her in the classroom. In a manner typical of the counter-culture 1960s in West Germany, she has reorganized the structure of the classroom, moving the chairs into a circle so as to undermine self-consciously the authoritarian structure of the class. After being left empty by others in the class, one of the seats next to her is finally taken by Rubinstein. Rubinstein, who is secretly attracted to the teacher in a clearly pubescent manner, is rewarded by her holding his hand. Suddenly all the male students want to sit next to her, and Rubinstein, flustered by the attention given him by her and his classmates, is inspired to hold an auction for the seat to give everyone in the class a chance. Eventually one of the students bids a hundred marks and Rubinstein, still confused by the teacher's actions, gives up his seat to him. The victor's response is to comment: "No sooner does a German woman hold his hand than Rubinstein auctions her off to the one who offers the most money. Now I understand how you get your money" (9). Rubinstein is taken aback as his offer of sharing the attention of the teacher is now read as a typically Jewish act. Torn by his unacceptable attraction for his teacher, who is both an authority figure and a non-Jew, his own sexuality is exposed as "Jewish." He quickly offers to donate the money to a good cause. His tormentor suggests giving it to the synagogue fund!

The central theme in Seligmann's novel is the confusing juxtaposition of Jewishness and male sexuality—each coming to represent the other. Rubinstein's impotence in the face of non-Jewish women; his complex, sexualized, but nonrealized relationship with Jewish women; even his attempted seduction by his teacher and his eventual relationship with the daughter of a former member of the SS—all relate to this confusion between sexual identity and the essence of Jewishness. At its core lies the very body of the Jew. In one of the central passages of the novel, Rubinstein tries to understand what exactly makes him different, what exactly makes him a Jew. It

is Sabbath morning and Rubinstein is sitting in the Reichenbach
Synagogue in Munich:

> Why do I even come here? What do I have in common with these
> people? That we are all members of the covenant with the Lord?
> What does that really mean? Our forefathers had their religion,
> their teaching, and tradition. And we? What do we have? The
> "covenant" has become degraded to a community of the circum-
> cised. German Jewry has, so to speak, come down to the prick.
> The covenant with the Lord now consists of a long chain of sacri-
> ficed foreskins. And what do I have from these sacrifices? A more
> sensitive prick, nothing else. Maybe that's the reason I spend the
> whole day thinking about nothing but my cock. The other guys
> in my class do the same thing. And in spite of that I am different.
> Only because my foreskin is missing? That's where it begins. The
> goyim supply the rest. (89–90)

Here, too, circumcision marks the Jewish male body and psyche
as different and provides a different relationship to the female, both
Jewish and non-Jewish.

Here one can contrast, for the moment, the different reception
of a writer such as Seligmann and one such as Dische from the standpoint of a gendered reading of both texts. Elvira Grözinger, writing
in the Jewish left-wing periodical *Semit*, sees this novel by Seligmann
as a sign of the perverse fascination of the German (non-Jewish here)
for the Jew. She casts this fascination in the most striking of images:
"When a Jew drops his underwear, all of the non-Jews stare with
interest, if not with fascination, and [Seligmann] drops his pants often and willingly. A pseudo-literary peepshow. Psychotherapists call
this the anal, oedipal or—in the best case—the oral phase. One could
suppose, however, narcissism or Jewish self-hatred."[56] Elvira
Grözinger's view of Dische is, however, quite different. She praises
Dische's work, especially the story "A Jewess for Charles Allen," as
an example of dealing with such questions without the gendered
"obsessiveness" she sees in the writings of Seligmann and Maxim
Biller, whose work will be discussed below. It is also clear that for
Grözinger, Dische does not have to expose her sexual difference. As
a woman, this difference is already inscribed on her body. But it is

not inscribed as a Jewish woman, only as a woman. "Dropping her pants" would not expose the Jewishness of the writer's obsession, only her indistinguishability from "German" women.

A clear contrast to this theme in the younger generation of Jewish writers in Germany can be found in Jurek Becker's novel, *Bronstein's Children* (1986). This was Becker's first return to a "Jewish" theme after his forced immigration to West Berlin from the German Democratic Republic in 1977.[57] Becker, a child-survivor of the Lodz ghetto, came to Berlin (East) with his father immediately after the war and was raised in the German Democratic Republic. He was expelled following the Wolf Biermann controversy. *Bronstein's Children* is without a doubt the most successful work he has written in the West. With the original title "How I Became a German," the novel traces two years in the formation of a young Jew in the German Democratic Republic from the perspective of his growing sense of his own conflicts of identity. The plot deals with a family—a father, his eighteen-year-old son, and grown daughter, and their lives in East Berlin in 1973 and 1974.

The "hero," or at least, the narrator of the novel, is the son, Hans, who recounts the story a year after the death of his father, Arno, in 1973. He attempts to reconstruct the events leading up to that event and to understand how he has been constructing his life since then. Becker provides a representation of the way a Jewish identity developed in Germany (here the GDR) in those individuals who had no firsthand experience of the Shoah but whose parents (and here, sibling) survived.

Jurek Becker's description, at the very beginning of the novel, of Hans as an athlete forms an epiphany which illuminates the rest of the text in a manner uncomprehended by the narrator until the conclusion of the work. Hans must complete the swimming test in order to graduate from high school, and his lack of interest in doing so reflects one of the images of the Jew in German fiction, the Jew as attempting to avoid any type of physical exertion. One is reminded of the Zionist leader Max Nordau's fin-de-siècle call for Jews to reform their bodies and become "New Muscle Jews" in order to become the physical equal of the Aryans. And yet Becker plays with

this standard theme much more consciously than he did in any of
his earlier "Jewish" novels.

The scene is set. Hans must take his swimming test and is ordered by one of his schoolmates, in a schoolboy Prussian tone, to
take off his swimsuit and shower before entering the pool. Hans's
answer is to punch him in the nose, to which the boy responds, after
getting up, that "he's crazy" (43). The reader is led into the resulting
uproar by the teachers who flood into the locker room and attempt
to provide a rationale for the incident. The explanation, imagined
by Hans to be whispered to his victim by the teacher, is that he's a
Jew. "There are slight sensitivities, which we cannot so easily comprehend" (47). The implication is that Hans did not want to remove
his swimsuit because of his physical difference, because of his circumcised penis. The chapter ends, however, with the revelation, in
the narrator's interior monologue, that he is not circumcised. He had
no hidden "Jewish" motivation (in his own understanding of this)
to hit his schoolmate, only an objection to his schoolmate's pedantic,
Prussian tone. Jews, according to Hans's account of Arno's view,
are an invention of those who wish to victimize those labeled as
Jews. Their Jewishness is *not* inscribed on their bodies, only in the
minds of the non-Jews. Circumcision is an illusion, a projection onto
the Jews by the Germans in the novel. This powerful scene reveals
the reactive moment in Becker's characters; their Jewishness is revealed only in their response to the corrupt world about them. Or so
we are led to believe by Hans.

Becker's theme is the inherent similarity of the Jewish body to
all bodies of the other inhabitants of Germany. It is a theme that
haunts the survivor-author. In what is undoubtedly the most complex and controversial novel by such an author, Edgar Hilsenrath's
The Nazi and the Barber (1973), the metamorphosis of the Nazi camp
guard Max Schulz into his murdered Jewish childhood friend Itzig
Finkelstein is the result of two operations.[58] (The novel's working
title had been "The Circumcised One.") The irony in Hilsenrath's
novel is that the German camp guard "looks Jewish," according to
Nazi racial theory, and his friend, the Jew, "looks Aryan." This is
not enough to save the latter's life, but the former can transform

himself into a "Jew" after the fall of the Third Reich. He goes to a Nazi doctor in 1945 and the doctor "remove[d] my SS tattoo from below my left arm—a pretty unsightly tattoo, a small letter denoting my blood type—then, his withered hands trembling, lined up my penis, trying to hold it steady, and sliced off the foreskin, performing a last service of love for Führer and Fatherland" (157). It is the "bent nose" and "circumcised member" that identifies this "new" Jew in the culture in which he finds himself (168). According to Hilsenrath, what makes the Jew are the externals of the body as read by the culture in which the Jew is literally "seen" (whether that culture is German or Israeli). Circumcision has no greater meaning. After the fall of the Wall, even Hilsenrath alters his view. In his most recent novel, *Jossel Wassermann's Homecoming* (1993), Hilsenrath spins the long, complicated life story of an Eastern European Jew whose death in Switzerland on the eve of the beginning of World War II heralds the destruction of his countrymen in the camps.[59] How Jossel Wassermann, an inadvertent hero during World War I, got to Switzerland and to safety is related to the significance of circumcision. After bribing some small-time hoodlums to row him across Lake Lugano, Jossel is knocked unconscious by them, stripped, and thrown into the water. He manages to reach the shore but is ashamed of his nakedness. After morning comes, he spies an Eastern European Jew on the beach and approaches him. Jossel's circumcised penis is the visual signal that leads to his rescue and the beginnings of his fortune in Switzerland, where he eventually dies a rich man. Here the public visibility of circumcision is an index for the Jew. In Hilsenrath's earlier, preunification view, it was a false sign of Jewishness. As the Jew becomes less and less visible in reality, so much the more must the literary representation of the Jew become visible.

This theme is drawn into question when the Jew is no longer the antithesis of the German, for the Jewish body is no longer the hallmark of difference. The skin color of the Turk or the Sri Lankan seems a more visible and more overt marker than the hidden mark of Jewish difference. This difference is hidden, not only because of the act of circumcision and the covering of the genitalia, but because it comes to represent the invisibility of the Jew in German culture. To overcome this invisibility, the literary figure of the Jew in such texts as these, *must* be circumcised and this fact made visible to the reader.

The question of the politics of circumcision among Jews in Germany is accentuated in the recent work of Maxim Biller. Biller, born in 1960 in Prague, emigrated to the Federal Republic in 1970. Biller is not only a widely read (and very controversial) columnist, but his volume of short stories struck his younger Jewish and non-Jewish contemporaries in Germany as the most "authentic" representation of the "negative symbiosis" that marks Jewish life in contemporary Germany. This claim for the authenticity of the writer's experience echoes the notion that these writers represent a "real" and "new" Jewish voice that reveals an experience unavailable to the German reader except in this context. Hannelore Schlaffer, in a long review of Biller's volume of essays, evokes Norman Mailer, Woody Allen, and American Jazz as models for Biller's "merging with his object."[60] Authenticity can be understood on both sides only as that which comes from outside the culture. And contemporary American culture, with its heavy Jewish overlay, at least for German readers, is the cutting edge of the postmodern. But for Schlaffer, Biller's world lacks any nuances; it consists of "friends or enemies," and this perceived split permits the masochistic contract to be written between the German reader and the Jewish author.

Maxim Biller's volume of short stories on the experience of Jewish life in the Germany of 1990 contains reflections on the ambiguity associated with making the Jew's body. Biller sees himself (or at least constructs his literary persona) after the model of another American Jewish writer, Joseph Heller, with whom he talks, in fantasy, about "literature, sex, and Judaism."[61] Thus, the definition of the cultural Jew is linked in his imagination (or at least the imagination of his literary voice) with the sexuality of the Jew. But it also represents the analogous position in German culture that he would like to have—a Jewish writer on contemporary Jewish topics within the mainstream of German cultural life. In his short story "Betrayal," Biller presents the central problem of Jurek Becker's work: "How can you make a Jew?" or, perhaps better stated, "How does the world make Jews?" Like Becker, Biller sees the construction of the Jew's body and his sexual identity as central to his argument. But for Biller, as for most of the writers of this postsurvivor generation, the question of the "reality" of a Jewish experience is not dismissed as merely part of the fantasy of the "Germans." Biller's story stands in a literary tradition which reflects the fascination of fin-de-siècle Jewish writers, such as Mynona (Salomo Friedländer), with the "operated Goy" or with the question: How one can make a Jewish body out of that of a non-Jew?[62] Central to both undertakings is the meaning of circumcision—circumcision not only of the penis but of the heart (following the Christian model of internalization of circumcision).

The protagonist of Biller's tale "Betrayal," Hugo Niehouß, a young journalist, discovers the meaning of his own, uncircumcised body during his first homosexual encounter. He asks his partner, whose penis is circumcised, whether he is Jewish. (He retrospectively comments that "this was, without a doubt, a very intense form of projection" [188].) His partner replied that "naturally" he wasn't a Jew, rather he had had himself circumcised for medical reasons. "Niehouß heard in his answer a sense of embarrassment. At that point he still had his foreskin, and that was exactly the reason why he suddenly felt so subordinate to this SS hunk—he had, if you want, seen the dead end." Niehouß articulates his anxiety about his difference in terms of the essential model of difference in the world in which he lives—after the Shoah it is the Jew who is the icon of difference. The anxiety about being seen as Jewish is heightened by the sense of self-awareness of the Jew's body. If one felt like a Jew, one's body had to be marked, had to be different—especially as this revealed the Jew within. For Niehouß acts "Jewish," that is, he play-acts the guilt of the German by taking the role of the Jew. He goes to Israel to work on a Kibbutz, wears a Jewish star, even brings matzos into his home at Passover. But all of these are signs of intense identification that grow out of a German guilt for the Shoah. They are the assumption of a role that he "knows" is but a role. These activities make his non-Jewish father very uncomfortable. It seems that the Jew within his son wants out. Once Niehouß is told by his father

that his mother, Lea Sonnenson, was a Jewish survivor, he is suddenly able to articulate his sense of difference, an essential difference which he feels was the root of his generalized alienation from
the world in which he lived. Teenage identity questions suddenly
become understood as Jewish identity questions. Five weeks after
he is told of his mother's Jewish identity by his father, he has himself
circumcised by a *mohel* (ritual circumciser) at the Jewish Hospital
(191). This change of the body seems to define for Niehouß an existing sense of difference he always had within. Now it has a focus, a
meaning beyond himself. He is not only circumcised but suddenly
loves to speak with a Jewish accent (*jiddeln*) (192). He suffers from
"Jewish self-hatred" as diagnosed by the narrative voice of the piece:
His is no longer an undifferentiated neurotic self-loathing, it now
has a basis in the historical world in which he lives, the world of the
Jew in Germany after the *Churban*, the destruction of the Jews of
Europe. Niehouß rejects his Jewishness in becoming a Jew, casting
his Jewish survivor mother totally out of his life. For unlike the Jew
within, the Jew without could be exorcised and distanced. How the
body itself comes to be understood is stressed in the tale. Niehouß
becomes a journalist, a "Jewish" profession, and is chosen by the
visible, Jewish literary critic of the magazine on which he works as
his successor. Threatening letters result, claiming that he got his
position only because of "his half-naked prick" (195). The circumcision of the gay male with whom Niehouß identified, the fantasy
about the Jewish conspiracy as related to a foreskin, all of this masks
the presence of his mother's body, the real root of his Jewish identity
in the tale. The story ends when he and his mother see one another
on a street in Munich after a four-year separation and each one
chooses to ignore the other's presence. He sees her reflected in the
window of a book shop where a display of books on the Shoah merge
with her image. He has become, in his mother's and his own estima-
tion, a "smart-mouthed, self-assured Jew" (198). A public persona,
as the narrator acknowledges, is not possible for his mother, who
has concealed her Jewishness. Her secretiveness is unfathomable to
anyone, including her son, who has not experienced the Shoah. But
his new visibility leads only to a neurotic self-loathing on his part.

In a later tale, "Glasses, Lara, and the Bells of St. Ursula," Biller incorporates a parallel moment. When the Jewish protagonist's non-Jewish girlfriend speaks to him about his "circumcised member" while stroking him, his response is not erotic but is to turn away from her. And her eyes "suddenly turn in upon themselves" (214) when she realizes that his circumcised penis now reflects his self-doubt. The centrality of the act of circumcision in Biller's world can be seen when he constructs the voice of a Jewish woman in his tale of the seemingly hypochondriac "Cilly," whose Russian boyfriend's uncircumcised "elephant trunk" (145/158) leads directly to her death from heart failure. (She makes love with him even after having been warned against such intense actions by her physician.) The Jewish woman's attraction to the uncircumcised member marks her awareness of the meaning of circumcision as a sign that the Jewish male is undesirable as a sexual partner. Her attraction stresses the difference of the Russian and his animal-like sexuality, represented by the uncircumcised penis. Throughout Biller's world, circumcision defines identity, but it also defines pathology. It comes to be a sign of the nature of the soul inscribed on the body. That all of Biller's Jewish protagonists are teenagers or young adults is not incidental. For the essential ambivalence about a sense of self at this stage of identity formation and the impact of an awareness of the meaning of the Jewish body are both present.

Biller's image of the body of the gay male is based on the internalized sense of difference of the uncircumcised Jew. It is striking to an American reader that it is the circumcised penis that is attractive because it is exotic in the German gay community while it is the "uncut" male who is deemed attractive in the circumcised world of the American gay community. The autobiography of Andreas Sinakowski, *The Interrogation* (1991), is one of the few contemporary German texts that link Jewish and gay identity.[63] Born in Berlin (East) in 1960, he was a member of the Secret Police (Stasi) of the former German Democratic Republic from 1979 to 1985, when he received official permission to leave the country for West Berlin. Sinakowski's ghost-written volume is one of a spate of recent self-revelatory autobiographies by citizens of the German Democratic Republic, including the former head of the Stasi, Markus Wolf. Sinakowski left the GDR prior to its collapse, and his text is a self-declared attempt to establish himself in the world of contemporary pan-German gay literature as a double victim of a repressive system, a system which permitted him little choice but to be an internal (and quite "official") spy.

It is fascinating that the "Jewish" aspect of Sinakowski's identity is marginalized in his autobiographical account, yet it constantly reappears to mark his self-definition as a victim. He sees himself (at least in 1991) as a struggling gay writer who happens to be Jewish. His autobiographical narrative, however, places his Jewish identity at the core of his desire to conform. In the opening chapter, Sinakowski positions himself as a Jew who is drawn into the net of the Stasi because of the anti-Semitism of the world in which he lives. An anti-Semitism of word and deed, of macabre "Auschwitz" jokes and anti-Semitic calls of "Hep! hep!" frame his world (14-16). The reality of these experiences is denied, however, by the party secretary in the school he attends, and he is told not to be so sensitive and to be concerned about the reputation of his school. This, according to his narrative, drives him to meet with his Stasi control and to prove that he really belongs in the GDR. His narrative moves from his sense of his role as a victim of anti-Semitism to his sense of vulnerability as a gay man. These ideas merge in his image of the victim. Sinakowski lives "in the beautiful land of burnt flesh" populated by old Nazis (18). It is a world which "praised Hitler yesterday" (63). But the world of Hitler is specifically the world "which banned all Jews out of its realm of power" (87). It is not the image of the gay which marks the victim of the Nazis, but the image of the Jew. Sinakowski's irony aims at the specific denial of the Shoah, a Shoah defined in terms of the murder of the Jews: "Privately, fifty percent were always against it. Privately, after the war about twenty million Germans had hidden 2.5 Jews. . . . Privately, Marika Rökk has always been against the persecution of the Jews. Privately, my friends always knew about 'it.' Privately, they never knew anything about it" (97-98). What is missing in Sinakowski's account of his life, especially in his detailed description of his sexual experiences, is anything that differentiates his own body from that of the other gay men he meets and with whom he sleeps. His body is a gay body, not a Jewish body. His solidarity is as a gay East German, even though, given the antifascist rhetoric of the GDR, he uses the image of the persecution of the Jews as his metaphoric frame. He presents himself as the gay victim of the Stasi, just as the Jews were the victims of the Nazis. The two worlds remain separate as Sinakowski focuses on establishing his credentials as a gay writer in the new Germany.

The problem of being a male Jewish writer in German extends into the world of contemporary Austrian writing. No one represents the "negative symbiosis" of Jews with contemporary "German" society in a more brittle way than the Viennese poet-novelist Robert Schindel. Schindel was born in 1944 and was hidden in occupied Vienna after his parents were sent to Auschwitz. In the early 1990s, the political situation in Austria, with Kurt Waldheim as president, became emblematic of a world so tolerant of the past that it made the life of Jews in Austria untenable in the present. Even Sinakowski evokes this in his autobiography (108). In his best-selling novel *Born* (1992), Schindel depicts the lives of two men who are "born" into specific roles—the sons of a survivor and a high Nazi functionary.[64] Like Seligmann, Schindel makes the body of the male Jew central to his understanding of the contortions Jewish males must find necessary to function in a contemporary Austria in which the old, anti-Semitic rhetoric is ubiquitous. He notes, for example, his Jewish protagonist's memory of his non-Jewish girlfriend: "He remembered that Käthe, during her first night in Vienna, said the thing about him that pleased her best was his racial sign (*Rassenmerkmai*). He had laughed and thought about his circumcised penis, but she brushed her finger teasingly over his nose. Then he embraced her and explained, while kissing her, that it wasn't a racial sign and that the Jews weren't a race and so on" (137). But the Jews are a "race" in the eyes of the Austrians in that they are literally seen as distanced and different.

For the Jewish writer, this difference becomes part of the literary sensitivity of the Jew, part of his manner of representing the world in which he lives, a difference experienced by the "blond mother's son" as "sedimentary bone-Hebrew" (*sedimentiertes Knochenhebräisch* [14]). This difference is inscribed by the culture particularly in the language of the Jew. The Jews speak differently, they have a "special relationship to language." This difference, like their internalization of the meaning of circumcision, shapes the way they see the world. When Jews are among themselves, they mock those Jews who are "Judeocentric" by "contorting their mouths and speaking with a Jewish accent" (*mauschelnd* [142]). And the Jewish protagonist with his pure German, the German that is the novelist's tool, is given to understand that his language, too, is different: "'What does that mean, that my language has something Jewish in it? I write a perfect German.' 'That's how you are different from the Germans. In contrast to them, you have to prove it'" (275). The internalized sense of the difference of the Jew's circumcised body goes along with the difference of the writer.

The topos of circumcision as the sign of the problematic identity of Central European Jewry after the Shoah appears within other extra-German literary contexts. Simon Louvish, the brilliant Anglo-Israeli novelist, has presented the self-image of the "mad" Hungarian Jew, Yerachmiel Farkash-Fenschechter; this character's life as "Friedrich Nietzsche" in a Jerusalem asylum is one focus of the first volume of Louvish's Avrom Blok trilogy written in the late 1980s. (Here the "mad" Jew has so internalized the world which tried to destroy him in the Shoah that he becomes "Friedrich Nietzsche," the very philosopher claimed by his tormentors as their mentor.) The self-representation associated with the act of circumcision is given an historical context in the novel: "By the time the Kecskemét mohel was cutting into the poor babe's ding dong the old order in Europe had crumbled." In an ironic aside, Louvish offers his microhistory of the meanings ascribed to circumcision as seen from an Israeli perspective:

> [Circumcision] was widespread in Pharaonic Egypt, they say. The Lord said to Abraham: "And ye shall circumcise the flesh of your foreskin, and it shall be a token of the covenant between me and you." "Sure, sure, Boss," said Abe, who had been promised a profusion of goodies. Siggy Freud, on the other hand, laid the blame

on Moses, and blew the gaffe on the whole damn schmeer: "Circumcision," said he, "is the symbolic substitute for the castration
which the primal father once inflicted upon his sons in the pleni-
tude of his absolute power, and whoever accepted that symbol
was showing by it that he was prepared to submit to the father's
will, even if it imposed the most painful sacrifice on him." But
some anthropologists said it derived from the clipping of the vine,
without which it would bear no fruit. A wag in Jerusalem's
Ta'amon Café, though, had the last word on the issue, claiming
Jewish boys were circumcised so that their foreskins should not
get caught in their zips.[65]

The theological-historical discourse about circumcision mirrored in
Louvish's microhistory is, of course, ironic. His answer to circumcision is to dismiss it as trivial—circumcision is a practical social necessity given the "modern" replacement of buttons with zippers.
For Louvish, neither Abraham nor Sigmund Freud has the answer
to the centrality of Jewish male sexuality for the self-image of the
male Jew. It is neither ritual nor repression. Louvish understands
the importance of the act of circumcision for Central European Jewish males—it made them into Jews even as unwilling infants and
marked that sign of difference onto their bodies. And that sign came
to be a sign of sexual difference, for the Jew in Europe was traditionally seen as sexually deviant.

The theme of circumcision-as-problem projected into German
culture reappears in the satire *The God-Fearer* (1992) by the
Anglo-South African Jewish writer Dan Jacobson. Jacobson, following the lead of Clive Sinclair, postulates a lost world in which it is
the Jews rather than the "Christers" who are in a majority and whose
constant persecution leads to a "Christer" Holocaust.[66] This inverted
fable is set in the imagined land of Ashkenaz, the world of Central
European Jewry with its ghettos and clearly marked Other. But the
Christers are marked by "the shaven faces of their men folk" as well
as by "the shamelessly uncut prepuces concealed within every pair
of Christian breeches. One of the prizes of a successful pursuit of a
Christer urchin was that you and your chums then had the opportu-
nity to pull down his lower garment and to gaze your full, with
fascination and disbelief, at the strange elongated, faceless, worm-

like object thus revealed." Here the sign of "how different they were from the majority" is hidden and yet reflected in their shaven faces. Jacobson, like Louvish, sees this as a quality of the difference of the Jews of Central Europe, a mark that was read as a sign of their inferiority.

Jacobson's and Louvish's image reflects a Central European tradition concerning the inherent nature of Jewish sexuality as corrupt and corrupting. The definition of the Jew as a member of the covenant—one who is circumcised—places the focus on the nature of Jewish male sexuality in a unique manner. The Jewish male's psyche, like his body, is different. This is an ancient topos harking back to Tacitus's description of the Jews as the "projectissima ad libidinem gens"—the most sensual of peoples. By the end of the nineteenth century, this view had become part of medical-forensic literature in Germany. The nature of the Jew was described as follows, for example, in one of the standard forensic studies of the time: "Further it must be noted that the sexuality of the Semitic race is in general powerful, yes, often greatly exaggerated."[67] Or as John S. Billings, leading American student of Jewish illness and head of the Surgeon General's Library in Washington, noted, when Jewish males are integrated into Western culture they "are probably more addicted to . . . sexual excesses than their ancestors were."[68] The physiognomy of the "sexual" male, like the representation of the Jew in modern culture, is "dark" (Biérent); he has a "dark complexion" (Bouchereau) or "brown skin" and a "long nose" (Mantegazza).[69] Jewish physicians of the period understood the implications of this charge. The Viennese Jewish physician Hanns Sachs, who was involved in the earliest development of psychoanalysis, commented in his memoirs on this version of the "timeworn prejudice that the Jewish . . . mind was abnormally preoccupied with matters of a sexual nature."[70] Some Jewish scientists of the fin de siècle, such as the Munich neurologist Leopold Löwenfeld, were forced to confront this charge and were unable to dismiss it. Löwenfeld argued, in a study of sexual constitution published in 1911, that the role of racial predisposition in structuring sexual drives can be confused by the mediating role that climate, nutrition, or culture can play.[71] But he and Jewish contemporaries such as Iwan Bloch have no doubt that racial identity does play some role in structuring sexual constitution. Others, like one of the original founders of the Vienna Psychoanalytic Association and Sigmund Freud's Jewish lodge brother Eduard Hitschmann, believed that "neuroses, psychoses, suicides, etc., play a more important role among the Jews, . . . they have many more sexual experiences than others and—a fact that must be particularly emphasized—take them much more seriously."[72] The Jews' mental states, specifically the psychopathologies associated with the Jews, are closely linked to their intense sexuality.

The Jew as Child Abuser and Circumcision as Child Abuse

The psychopathologies associated with the Jews differ from culture to culture over time. With the widespread practice of surgical circumcision in post-Shoah America, the circumcised penis is no longer an absolute mark of Jewish difference. In post-Shoah Germany (both East and West and united) it remains a sign of the male Jewish body. (The exoticism of the circumcised gay male is simply a romantic reversal of this image within a highly marginalized social group.) Great Britain, where Simon Louvish now lives and works, is in an intermediate position concerning the ubiquitousness of infant male circumcision. The British circumcise their male infants more frequently than the Germans but less frequently than the Americans. Post-Shoah Germany remains a culture where circumcision is not only a mark of difference but one that continues to be associated with the older, negative tradition of the perverse sexuality of the Jews.

This can be seen, for example, in the discourse about circumcision in the most recent book by the widely read and widely respected German psychoanalyst Alice Miller. Miller, long a resident of Switzerland, broke with traditional psychoanalysis over the issue of the reality of trauma as the origin of neurosis. Like Sándor Ferenczi at the end of his life, she argued that Freud was wrong in abandoning the seduction theory. In her 1988 book *Banished Knowledge: Facing Childhood Injuries*, she argues that *"crimes against children represent the most frequent of all types of crime."* "Child abuse" is not, however, only the physical and psychological maltreatment of children. It extends for her into the realm of the adult's treatment of the child's body, "the actual physical mutilation of small children," and thus into a devastating critique of "the cruel mutilation of children's sexual organs."[73] Over three pages, she cites the American anthropologist Desmond Morris's attack on male infant circumcision.[74] He traces the tradition of circumcision from its religious roots through its medicalization as a therapy against masturbatory insanity and the predisposition of the uncircumcised penis to cancer of the penis. Alice Miller sees this as a form of torture: "What eventually happens to the person who was mutilated as a child? When a small child is tortured by ignorant adults, won't he have to take his revenge later in life?" The form of this revenge is very specific for Alice Miller.

For Miller it is a "fictitious claim that circumcision is performed in the interests of the child"[75]—the standard defense of the wide-scale practice of infant male circumcision within the medical profession. Rather, it "constitutes a cruelty that will later encourage the adult to indulge in similar, also denied cruelties and will invest his deeds with the legitimacy of a clear conscience." Here the attack on surgical circumcision is an attack on the psychological results of the practice for every circumcised male child. Circumcision is "outlandish behavior" that "mutilates" children. Even when circumcision is a religious obligation, it remains a "cruelty . . . because of the ignorance of the priests." What happens to this "mutilated" male child in society? "He is bound to avenge himself." This revenge is inflicted on the children of the "abused" individual in the form of the repetition of the act, but even more so these "victims" can also become "criminals." For Alice Miller, all criminals were once victims. Only the individual who can "confront his own past" can be freed from this asocial action.

Miller's rhetoric about circumcision has its own tradition within modern psychology. In 1950, Erik H. Erikson, the late German Jewish psychoanalyst, saw the ritual of circumcision among the Jews as the way the Jew "'asked for it.'"[76] "It" in this context is the unwanted attention of the anti-Semite which led to the Shoah. This view has its oblique roots in Sigmund Freud's own association of circumcision with the continuity of anti-Semitism in his 1938 study *Moses and Monotheism*.[77] But in post-Shoah Germany, any such direct labeling of circumcision as a Jewish problem would be taboo. Rather, Miller's view is very similar to the radical feminist critique of Judaism, found in Germany during the 1980s, as the ultimate patriarchal religion.[78] The Jew is rarely mentioned, but all of the associations of the older, anti-Semitic representation of the Jew are attributed to "religious patriarchy." The assumptions in this representation of the Jew are in keeping with the earlier images of the Jews as the font of all evil, ideas that have haunted German conceptions of the Jew in the past and present. In a famous case of media censorship in 1979, the West German television authorities were forbidden to broadcast a program on anti-Semitism in the Black Forest; in the program, one of those interviewed referred to Jews globally as "circumcised fools."[79] In Miller's text, too, the discourse about the Jewish male body as the representation of all "evil, destructiveness, and perversion" represents this continuity with the past. While not all males are thought of as circumcised, all Jewish males are. The social category of the Jewish male consists exclusively of damaged and abused individuals, who themselves damage and abuse. German-speaking Jewish males confront this attitude toward their own body, and therefore their own psyche, at every turn in German culture. They are different and this difference is embedded in the nature of their sexuality.

In a European context, the male Jew is labeled inherently different and corrupt. As we have seen in the fictions of Jewish, heterosexual males, circumcision defines the Jewish male—even within his own fantasy. The central image is that of the male Jew (whether circumcised or not) as an abused child and therefore as an abusing adult. The abuse he inflicts is played out in two of the novels through a representation of the conflict between the generations, between Becker's and Seligmann's teenage males and their parents. This conflict is generally understood to be an essential part of a child's development, but in these texts, it is a reflection of the Jewish identity of the children. Becker's father figure, with his link to the Shoah and his revengeful nature, and the German Jewish parents in Seligmann's

novel are exemplars of the focus of any child's oedipal fantasies. But
here they are also Jews who have themselves been abused by the
entire society in which they dwell. They are damaged because of
their historical experience as victims and survivors. Miller can only
argue on the level of the individual, and circumcision becomes the
mark of the Jews' abuse of the Jews. It is clear that there are analogous discussions of male sexuality in the work of North American
writers such as Philip Roth and Mordechai Richler. But in their work
the obsessive focus on the physical difference of the male Jew as the
icon of the sexual difference ascribed to him is missing. Alexander
Portnoy's masturbatory fantasies and Joshua Shapiro's sexual difficulties are parodies of the sexual taboos associated with the representation of the Jew. (In Bernard Malamud's *The Assistant* [1957], the
relationship between the lack of circumcision and the brutal sexuality of the non-Jew arises in the context of the rape of a Jewish woman
by her father's non-Jewish "assistant." And it is resolved by the
rapist's expiation of his act by having himself circumcised and by
his conversion to Judaism.) These fictions represent the endogenous
sexual selectivity associated with the Jew in Jewish religious practice. For Anglo-Jewish writers, the image of circumcision as the key-
stone to the nature of the Jewish body seems to vanish. Clive Sinclair,
in his short story "The Promised Land," employs the metaphor of
circumcision to contrast his own sense of Diaspora identity and the
"true" Jewish identity of the Israeli:

> "Slicha, efor Rehov Gruniman?" I say to the locals, but cannot
> understand the reply. I don't blame Rivka, she didn't write the
> textbook after all, but outside the supermarkets my vocabulary is
> useless. There's one version of the Bible in which Moses attempts
> to extricate himself from God's command by stammering that his
> tongue is not circumcised. Well, that's exactly how I feel in Israel:
> I am Jewish, but my tongue is not circumcised. "Ani lo mdaber
> ivrit," I say. I do not speak Hebrew.[80]

The internalization of the circumcised Jew as the image of the true
Jew ironically presented here reflects the European tradition that
circumcision represents the essence of Jewish identity. This image,

which is of such great power within German culture that even Friedrich Schiller could evoke the image of the male Jew as having been born circumcised, reflects the need to make an absolute distinction between the nature of the Jew and that of the Aryan.[81] Parallel images are to be found in a recent Jewish context in German in Robert Schindel's novel *Born*, as well as in the short story "Betrayal" by Maxim Biller discussed above. Biller's protagonist's tongue is circumcised through the act of circumcision. Biller in no way evokes a simple biological reflex. Rather, the sign of circumcision reflects his protagonist's sudden self-consciousness of the Jewishness projected onto his character, even to his use of language.

The meaningful distinction between Jew and non-Jew resulting from the practice of infant male circumcision becomes less and less possible as the practice of circumcision becomes more and more widespread. Among Jews in Central Europe, as can be seen in the image evoked by Becker and Biller, the debate about the practice of circumcision reaches back to the 1840s, and the social practice of circumcision among Jews is by no means universal at the beginning of the twentieth century. Indeed, Samuel Holdheim, the most radical exponent of reformed Judaism, argued that circumcision was in no way to be understood as a necessity of male Jewish identity. This ambivalence became a touchstone for establishing the internalized sense of the Jewish male body. The primary means of avoiding these confrontations between notions of a good, healthy, uncircumcised body and an evil, ill, circumcised one was to understate the meaning of circumcision.

For the post-Shoah generation, circumcision becomes an external mark of difference defining the Jewish body within the body politic. Authors such as Becker, Biller, and Seligmann can evoke this difference without any hesitation as the mark of their characters' sense of isolation and distance from the Aryan body. The culture in which they live remains permeated with an intense sense of the difference of the Jew. Indeed, a recent survey established that one German in every eight holds anti-Semitic attitudes.[82] But in evoking this anxiety about their own identity, these authors also call into question the difference of the Jewish body as a marker of their own iden-

tity. Through their projection of the image of the damaged body of
the Jew into their fictive creations, they enable the reader to see this
difference (and to judge its internalization). The readers' judgments—like the authors'—draw the self-doubt of the Jewish male
into question, or at least frame it within the narrative tradition of
adolescent development. Biller, Becker, and Seligmann argue for
acculturation. They see the creation of a new sense of Jewish identity in the new Germany not as desirable but as necessary. Unlike
Henryk Broder and Lea Fleischmann in the 1980s, they do not advocate a removal of the Jew from German culture. Whether Jews in the
United States or Israel approve of this development or not, whether
non-Jewish Germans are aware of this or not, there is a new sense of
Diaspora Jewish identity evolving within Germany. Thus, Jewish
writers, especially male writers, need to call into question the difference of the Jew as represented in Alice Miller's work. It is this difference which these authors inscribe on the bodies of their fictive characters so as to place in the foreground the implications of the Jewish
male body—their own bodies—in the struggle for a Jewish identity
in contemporary Germany.

Notes

Introduction

1. On the general question of the Jewish Diaspora, see Werner Keller, *Diaspora: The Post-Biblical History of the Jews*, trans. Richard and Clara Winston (London: Pitman, 1969); Rudolf Mosis, ed., *Exil, Diaspora, Rückkehr: Zum theologischen Gespräch zwischen Juden und Christen* (Düsseldorf: Patmos-Verlag, 1978); Joan Comay, *The Diaspora Story: The Epic of the Jewish People among the Nations* (London: Weidenfeld and Nicolson, 1981); Yosef Hayim Yerushalmi, *Zakhor, Jewish History and Jewish Memory* (Seattle: University of Washington Press, 1982); James Parkes, *End of an Exile: Israel, the Jews, and the Gentile World* (Marblehead, MA: Micah, 1982); John J. Collins, *Between Athens and Jerusalem: Jewish Identity in the Hellenistic Diaspora* (New York: Crossroads, 1983); Etan Levine, ed., *Diaspora: Exile and the Jewish Condition* (New York: J. Aronson, 1983); Jacob Neusner, *The Jewish War against the Jews: Reflections on Golah, Shoah, and Torah* (New York: Ktav, 1984); Arnold M. Eisen, *Galut: Modern Jewish Reflection on Homelessness and Homecoming* (Bloomington: Indiana University Press, 1986); Howard M. Sachar, *Diaspora: An Inquiry into the Contemporary Jewish World* (New York: Perennial Library, 1986); David Biale, *Power & Powerlessness in Jewish History* (New York: Schocken, 1987); John Bunzl, *Der lange Arm der Erinnerung: jüdisches Bewußtsein heute* (Vienna: Böhlau, 1987); Yitzhak F. Baer, *Galut*, trans. Robert Warshow (Lanham, MD: University Press of America, 1988); Walter P. Zenner, ed., *Persistence and Flexibility: Anthropological Perspectives on the American Jewish Experience* (Albany: State University of New York Press, 1988); Joseph Grunblatt, *Exile and Redemption: Meditations on Jewish History* (Hoboken, NJ: Ktav, 1988); Jacob Neusner, *Who, Where, and What Is "Israel"?: Zionist Perspectives on Israeli and American Judaism* (Lanham, MD: University Press of America, 1989); Marvin Lowenthal, *A World Passed By: Great Cities in Jewish Diaspora History* (Malibu, CA: J. Simon/Pangloss Press, 1990); Jacob Neusner, *Self-Fulfilling Prophecy: Exile and Return in the History of Judaism* (Atlanta: Scholars Press, 1990); *Eretz Israel, Israel, and the Jewish Diaspora: Mutual Relations*, ed. Menachem Mor (Lanham, MD: University Press of America, 1991); Eliezer Don-Yehiya, ed., *Israel and Diaspora Jewry: Ideological and Political Perspectives* (Ramat-Gan: Bar-Ilan University Press, 1991); Walter P. Zenner, *Minorities in the Middle: A Cross-Cultural Analysis* (Albany: State University of New York Press, 1991); David A. Teutsch, ed., *Imagining the Jewish Future: Essays and Responses* (Albany: State University of New York Press, 1992); Willem Cornelis van Unnik, *Das Selbstverständnis der jüdischen Diaspora in der hellenistisch-römischen Zeit* (Leiden: Brill, 1993).

2. Following the completion of the manuscript for this book, a won-
derful English anthology appeared, with works by contemporary Jewish
writers in German: *Jewish Voices, German Words: Growing Up Jewish in Post-
war Germany and Austria* (ed. Elena Lappin, trans. Krishna Winston [North
Haven, CT: Catbird Press, 1994]). The volume contains texts by Benjamin
Korn, Katja Behrens, Chaim Noll, Barbara Honigmann, Henryk M.
Broder, Esther Dischereit, Robert Menasse, Thomas Feibel, Maxim Biller, Rafael
Seligmann, Robert Schindel, Matthias Hermann, Peter Stephan Jungk, and
Leo Sucharewicz.

A selection of the published works of the writers mentioned in this
book is given here, unless a detailed examination of their work follows
later:

Ruth Beckermann, b. 1952

Unzugehoerig: Oesterreicher und Juden nach 1945 (Vienna: Loecker, 1989); *Im
blinden Winkel: Nachrichten aus Mitteleuropa* (Vienna: Brandstätter, 1985);
Die Mazzesinsel: Juden in der Wiener Leopoldstadt 1918-1938 (Vienna: Loecker,
1984).

Katja Behrens, b. 1942

Salomo und die anderen: Jüdische Geschichten (Frankfurt am Main: S. Fischer,
1993); ed., *Weiches Wasser bricht den Stein: Widerstandsreden* (Frankfurt am
Main: Fischer Taschenbuch Verlag, 1984); *Die dreizehnte Fee* (Frankfurt am
Main: Fischer Taschenbuch, 1983); *Im Wasser tanzen: ein Erzählzyklus* (Frankfurt am Main: Luchterhand, 1990); ed., *Abschiedsbriefe* (Düsseldorf: Claassen,
1987); *Von einem Ort zum andern: Erzählungen* (Pfaffenweiler: Pfaffenweiler
Presse, 1987); *Die weisse Frau: Erzählungen* (Frankfurt am Main: Suhrkamp,
1978); *Jonas: Erzählungen* (Pfaffenweiler: Pfaffenweiler Presse, 1981).

Ulla Berkéwicz

Engel sind schwarz und weiß (Frankfurt am Main: Suhrkamp, 1992); *Josef
Stirbt: Erzählung* (Frankfurt am Main: Suhrkamp, 1982); *Josef is dying*, trans.
Gerald Williams (Sausalito, CA: Post-Apollo Press, 1992); *Michel, sag ich*
(Frankfurt am Main: Suhrkamp, 1984); *Nur wir: ein Schauspiel* (Frankfurt
am Main: Suhrkamp, 1991).

Barbara Honigmann, b. 1949

Roman von einem Kinde: sechs Erzählungen (Darmstadt: Luchterhand, 1986);
Eine Liebe aus nichts (Berlin: Rowohlt, 1991).

Elfriede Jelinek, b. 1946

Wir sind Lockvögel Baby! (Reinbek bei Hamburg: Rowohlt, 1970); *Michael.
Ein Jugendbuch für die Infantilgesellschaft* (Reinbek bei Hamburg:
Rowohlt-Taschenbuch-Verlag, 1972); *Die Liebhaberinnen* (Reinbek bei Ham-
burg: Rowohlt, 1975); *Die Ausgesperrten* (Reinbek bei Hamburg: Rowohlt,
1980); *Ende: Gedichte von 1966-1968* (Schwifting: Schwiftinger
Galerie-Verlag, 1980); *Die endlose Unschuldigkeit: Prosa, Hörspiel, Essay*
(Schwifting: Schwiftinger Galerie-Verlag, 1980); *Was geschah, nachdem Nora
ihren Mann verlassen hatte?: acht Hörspiele*, ed. Helga Geyer-Ryan (Munich:
Deutscher Taschenbuch Verlag, 1982); *Die Klavierspielerin* (Reinbek bei
Hamburg: Rowohlt, 1983); *Theaterstücke*, ed. Ute Nyssen (Cologne:
Prometh-Verlag, 1984); *Oh Wildnis, oh Schutz vor ihr: Prosa* (Reinbek bei
Hamburg: Rowohlt, 1985); *Krankheit, oder, moderne Frauen* (Cologne:

Prometh-Verlag, 1987); *Lust* (Reinbek bei Hamburg: Rowohlt, 1989); *Wolken, Heim* (Göttingen: Steidl, 1990); *Totenauberg: ein Stück* (Reinbek bei Hamburg: Rowohlt, 1991).
    Ruth Klüger, b. 1931
weiter leben: eine jugend (Göttingen: Wallstein, 1992).
    Jeannette Lander, b. 1931
William Butler Yeats. Die Bildersprache seiner Lyrik (Stuttgart: Kohlhammer, 1967); *Ezra Pound* (Berlin: Colloquium Verlag, 1968); *Ein Sommer in der Woche der Itke K.* (Frankfurt am Main: Insel, 1971); *Die Töchter* (Frankfurt am Main: Insel, 1976); *Der letzte Flug* (Berlin: Literarisches Colloquium, 1978); *Ich, Allein* (Königstein/Ts.: Autoren-Edition, 1980); *Jahrhundert der Herren* (Berlin: Aufbau, 1993).
    Irene Runge
Sechs Wochen Jerusalem (Berlin: Reiher, 1990); *Onkel Max ist jüdisch: neun Gespräche mit Deutschen, die Juden halfen* (Berlin: Dietz, 1991).
    Robert Schindel, b. 1944
Gebürtig (Frankfurt am Main: Suhrkamp, 1992); *Ein Feuerchen im Hintennach: Gedichte, 1986-1991* (Frankfurt am Main: Suhrkamp, 1992); *Im Herzen die Krätze: Gedichte* (Frankfurt am Main: Suhrkamp, 1988); *Geier sind pünktliche Tiere: Gedichte* (Frankfurt am Main: Suhrkamp, 1987); *Ohneland: Gedichte vom Holz der Paradeiserbäume 1979-1984* (Frankfurt am Main: Suhrkamp, 1986).
    Peter Sichrovsky, b. 1947
Wir wissen nicht was morgen wird, wir wissen wohl was gestern war: junge Juden in Deutschland und Österreich (Cologne: Kiepenheuer & Witsch, 1985); *Strangers In Their Own Land: Young Jews in Germany and Austria Today*, trans. Jean Steinberg (London: Tauris, 1986); *Mein Freund David: ein Kinderroman* (Zurich: Nagel & Kimche, 1990); *Die Kinder Abrahams: Israels junge Generation* (Cologne: Kiepenheuer & Witsch, 1990); *Abraham's Children: Israel's Young Generation*, trans. Jean Steinberg (New York: Pantheon, 1991); *Schuldig geboren: Kinder aus Nazifamilien* (Cologne: Kiepenheuer & Witsch, 1987); *Born Guilty: The Children of the Nazis*, trans. Jean Steinberg (London: Tauris, 1988).
    The most detailed bibliography is that compiled annually by the owner of the Jewish Bookstores in Munich and Berlin, Rachel Salamander, under the title *Literatur zum Judentum*.

    3. See, for example, Irene Heidelberger-Leonhard, "'Auschwitz werden die Deutschen den Juden nie verzeihen.' Überlegungen zu Günter Kunerts Judesein," in Manfred Durzak and Hartmut Steinecke, eds., *Günter Kunert: Beiträge zu seinem Werk* (Munich: Carl Hanser, 1992), pp. 252-66, and John Shreve, *Nur wer sich ändert, bleibt sich treu: Wolf Biermann im Westen* (New York: Peter Lang, 1989).

    4. In this context, see Leslie A. Adelson, *Making Bodies, Making History: Feminism and German Identity* (Lincoln: University of Nebraska Press, 1993).

5. A recent conference in Munich was devoted to the topic of the new role of young Jews in Germany and the problems which they face in defining a Diaspora experience in the new Germany. See *Junge Juden in Deutschland: Protokoll einer Tagung* (Munich: Jugend und Kulturzentrum der israelitischen Kultusgemeinde München, 1991).

6. See Margrit Frölich, "Between Affluence and Rebellion: The Work of Thomas Brasch in the Interface between East and West" (Ph.D. diss., Cornell University, 1992).

7. Sandra Braude, *Windswept Plains* (Cape Town: Buschu, 1991), 79.

8. See the general discussion of the meaning of "Diaspora" and "Galut" in *Encyclopaedia Judaica*, 16 vols. (Jerusalem: Keter, 1972), 6:7-19 and 7:275-95.

9. The covenant formula can be found in Jer. 7:23, 11:4, 31:1 and Ezek. 11:20, 14:11, 37:23, 27.

10. See the insightful reading by Daniel and Jonathan Boyarin, "Diaspora: Generation and the Ground of Jewish Identity," *Critical Inquiry* 19 (1993): 693-725.

11. Richard Andree, *Zur Volkskunde der Juden* (Leipzig: Velhagen & Klasing, 1881), 24-25; translated from Maurice Fishberg, "Materials for the Physical Anthropology of the Eastern European Jew," *Memoirs of the American Anthropological Association* 1 (1905-7): 6-7.

12. Friedrich Delitzsch, *Babel und Bibel* (Leipzig: J. C. Hinrich, 1902), 10-11.

13. Gustav Janouch, *Conversations with Kafka*, trans. Goronwy Rees (London: Derek Verschoyle, 1953), 66-67.

14. Jacob Wassermann, *My Life as German and Jew* (London: George Allen & Unwin, 1933), 156.

15. Ibid.

16. Werner Sombart, *The Jews and Modern Capitalism*, trans. M. Epstein (Glencoe, IL: Free Press, 1951), 272.

17. Rudolf Virchow, "Gesamtbericht über die Farbe der Haut, der Haare und der Augen der Schulkinder in Deutschland," *Archiv für Anthropologie* 16 (1886): 275-475.

18. George L. Mosse, *Toward the Final Solution: A History of European Racism* (New York: Howard Fertig, 1975), 90-91.

19. Arthur Schnitzler, *Fräulein Else, a Novel*, trans. Robert A. Simon (New York: Simon and Schuster, 1925), 26-27.

20. Arthur Schnitzler, *Plays and Stories*, ed. Egon Schwarz (New York: Continuum, 1982), 256.

21. Georg Mannheimer, *Lieder eines Juden* (Prague: Neumann, 1937), 31. (My translation.)

22. This report was submitted to Congress on December 3, 1910, and issued on March 17, 1911. A full text was published by Columbia University Press in 1912. Boas summarizes his findings (and chronicles the objections to this report) in his *Race, Language and Culture* (New York: Macmillan, 1940), 60-75. An excellent reading of this problem is that of Carl N. Degler, *Culture versus Biology in the Thought of Franz Boas and Alfred L. Kroeber* (New York: Berg, 1989).

23. Boas, *Race*, 83.

24. Cited from an interview by Neal Gabler, *An Empire of Their Own: How the Jews Invented Hollywood* (New York: Crown, 1988), 242-43.

25. "Types," *The Jewish Encyclopedia*, 12 vols. (New York: Funk and Wagnalls, 1906), 12:295.

26. Heinrich Heine, *Werke*, ed. Klaus Briegleb, 12 vols. (Berlin: Ullstein, 1981), 7:31. (My translation.)

Jewish Self-Consciousness and Awareness of Jews in Post-Wall Germany

1. Quoted from the translation by Michael Bullock in Edward Mornin, ed., *Three Eerie Tales from 19th-century German* (New York: Ungar, 1975), 151. The original is now included in a critical edition by Walter Huge, Annette von Droste-Hülshoff, *Historisch-kritische Ausgabe*, vol. 5, pt. 1: *Prosa* (Tübingen: Max Niemeyer, 1978), 1-42. On the garbled Hebrew in the text, see Richard Hauschild, "Die Herkunft und Textgestaltung der hebräischen Inschrift in der 'Judenbuche' der Annette von Droste- Hülshoff," *Euphorion* 46 (1952): 85-99.

2. Philip Roth, "'I always wanted you to admire my fasting' or, Looking at Kafka" (1973), quoted from J. P. Stern, ed., *The World of Franz Kafka* (New York: Holt, Rinehart and Winston, 1980), 210.

3. On the complexities of this history, see *Die freundliche Zivilgesellschaft: Rassismus und Nationalismus in Deutschland,* ed. Redaktiondiskus (Berlin: ID Archiv, 1992); Erica Burgauer, *Zwischen Erinnerung und Verdrängung—Juden in Deutschland nach 1945* (rowohlts enzyklopaedie 532) (Reinbek bei Hamburg: Rowohlt, 1993); Gerhard Zwerenz, *Die Rückkehr des toten Juden nach Deutschland* (Ismaning bei Munich: Hueber, 1986); Jakob Josef Petuchowski, *On the Validity of German-Jewish Self-Definitions* (New York: Leo Baeck Institute, 1985); Jörg von Uthmann, *Doppelgänger, du bleicher Geselle: zur Pathologie des deutsch-*

jüdischen Verhältnisses (Munich: Knaur, 1983); Hans Israel Bach, *The German Jew: a Synthesis of Judaism and Western Civilization, 1730-1930* (Oxford: pub. for the Littman Library by Oxford University Press, 1984).

4. Esther Dischereit, *Merryn* (Frankfurt am Main: Suhrkamp, 1992), 117.

5. The term is from Dan Diner, "Negative Symbiose: Deutsche und Juden nach Auschwitz," *Babylon* 1 (1986): 9-20. On its applicability in the present context, see Jack Zipes, "Die kulturelle Operation von Deutschen und Juden im Spiegel der neueren deutschen Literatur," *Babylon* 8 (1990): 34-44; Klaus Briegleb, "Negative Symbiose," in Klaus Briegleb and Sigrid Weigel, eds. *Gegenwartsliteratur seit 1968* (Munich: Hanser, 1992), 117-52; Hans Schütz, *Juden in der deutschen Literatur* (Munich: Piper, 1992), 309-29.

6. Rafael Seligmann, *Mit beschränkter Hoffnung: Juden, Deutsche, Israelis* (Hamburg: Hoffmann und Campe, 1991), 97-98.

7. See Charlotte Kahn, "The Different Ways of Being a German," *Journal of Psychohistory* 20 (1993): 381-98.

8. *Die Zeit*, July 10, 1992, 8.

9. Ibid.

10. *The Financial Times*, December 2, 1992.

11. *New York Times*, August 10, 1993, A8.

12. *Washington Post* (National Edition), September 28–October 4, 1992, 17.

13. *New York Times*, August 10, 1993, A8.

14. *Washington Post* (National Edition), September 28–October 4, 1992, 26.

15. *New York Times*, August 10, 1993, A8.

16. *Die Tageszeitung*, May 7, 1990.

17. *New York Times*, June 6, 1993, A3.

18. *U.S. News & World Report*, March 1, 1993, 12.

19. *Der Spiegel*, 3-4 (March 1992): 52-66; 41-50.

20. *Die Tageszeitung*, July 10, 1989.

21. "'Es war keiner von uns,'" *Die Zeit*, September 7, 1990.

22. "Wieder jüdische Friedhöfe und Synagoge beschmiert," *Süddeutsche Zeitung*, May 23, 1990.

23. *Der Tagesspiegel,* May 6, 1990.

24. *Frankfurter Rundschau,* March 16, 1990, and *Die Tageszeitung,* March 16, 1990.

25. *New York Times,* October 12, 1993.

26. *New York Times,* November 23, 1992.

27. *Süddeutsche Zeitung,* August 27, 1993.

28. See my talk, "German Reunification and the Jews," *New German Critique* 52 (1991): 173-91.

29. *New York Times,* May 30, 1993, A1.

30. *New York Times,* May 31, 1993, A22.

31. *New York Times,* June 4, 1993, A3.

32. *New York Times,* June 4, 1993, A30.

33. *Washington Post,* March 5, 1993, A23.

34. *New York Times,* May 31, 1993, A6.

35. *Berliner Zeitung,* July 20, 1992.

36. Hans Jürgen Syberberg, *Vom Unglück und Glück der Kunst in Deutschland nach dem letzten Kriege* (Munich: Matthes & Seitz, 1990). The best study of this work in light of the culture of anti-Semitism in Germany is Eric Santner, "The Trouble with Hitler: Postwar German Aesthetics and the Legacy of Fascism," *New German Critique* 57 (1992): 5-24.

37. *New York Times,* August 10, 1993, A8.

38. A detailed overview of right-wing violence appeared in *Der Spiegel* 49 (July 1992): 14-32.

39. *Süddeutsche Zeitung,* December 2, 1992.

40. *Die Welt,* August 27, 1993.

41. See especially his *Über Ruhestörer: Juden in der deutschen Literatur* (Munich: dtv, 1993).

42. *Süddeutsche Zeitung,* October 13, 1989.

43. *Frankfurter Rundschau,* May 30, 1989 and *Süddeutsche Zeitung,* May 29, 1989.

44. *Berliner Morgenpost,* November 17, 1990.

45. *Der Tagesspiegel,* January 27, 1989.

46. *Berliner Zeitung,* October 11, 1991.

47. *Die Zeit,* February 2, 1990, 14.

48. *Frankfurter Rundschau,* February 10, 1990.

49. Sander L. Gilman, "Male Sexuality and Contemporary Jewish Literature in German: The Damaged Body as the Image of the Damaged Soul," *Genders* 16 (1993): 114-40.

50. Susannah Heschel, "Jüdisch-feministische Theologie und Antijudaismus in christlich-feministischer Theologie," in Leonore Siegele-Wenschkewitz, ed., *Verdrängte Vergangenheit, die uns bedrängt: Feministische Theologie in der Verantwortung für die Geschichte* (Munich: Chr. Kaiser, 1988), 54-103.

51. *Der Spiegel* 28 (June 1992): 55-69.

52. *Der Tagesspiegel,* August 6, 1993.

53. Micha Brumlik, *The Situation of the Jews in Today's Germany,* 1990 Paul Lecture (Bloomington: Jewish Studies Program of Indiana University, 1990).

Jewish Writing in Its German and Jewish Contexts

1. Primo Levi, *The Drowned and the Saved,* trans. Raymond Rosenthal (New York: Summit Books, 1988), 167-97.

2. Michael Wolffsohn, "Juden leben gern in Deutschland," *Die Welt,* April 25, 1992: 17.

3. Rafael Seligmann, *Mit beschränkter Hoffnung: Juden, Deutsche, Israelis* (Hamburg: Hoffmann und Campe, 1991), 112-13. The diary section on the negative reception of his first novel by the Jewish community in Germany was first published as "Kein Schalom Allerseits," *Semit* 2 (1990): 74-76.

4. See the discussion in Gilles Deleuze and Félix Guattari, *Kafka: Toward a Minor Literature,* trans. Dana Polan (Minneapolis: University of Minnesota Press, 1986), 66-67.

5. Jean-François Lyotard, *Heidegger et "les juifs"* (Paris: Galilée, 1988).

6. Chaim Noll, *Nachtgedanken über Deutschland* (Hamburg: Rowohlt, 1992).

7. Rafael Seligmann, *Israels Sicherheitspolitik: zwischen Selbstbehauptung und Präventivschlag, eine Fallstudie über Grundlagen und Motiv* (Munich: Bernard & Graefe, 1982).

8. See John Neubauer, *The fin-de-siècle Culture of Adolescence* (New Haven: Yale University Press, 1992).

9. Anon., "Muß man als Jude in Deutschland wahnsinning werden?" *Jüdische Zeitung*, May 13, 1988.

10. Seligmann, *Mit beschränkter Hoffnung*, 180-85.

11. Manya Gutman, "In Demut kleine Brötchen backen," *Allgemeine Zeitung der Juden in Deutschland*, March 24, 1989.

12. Manya Gutman, "Verordnete Zumutung," *Jüdische Zeitung*, February 1989.

13. Seligmann, *Mit beschränkter Hoffnung*, 149.

14. Henryk M. Broder, "Rubinsteins Beschwerden," *Die Zeit*, August 18, 1989.

15. Günther Fischer, "Rubinsteins Versteigerung," *Semit* 5 (1989): 34.

16. Elvira Grözinger, "Zwischen Exhibitionismus und Literatur: Von den Debütanden Seligmann, Biller, Dische und dem kleinen Unterschied," *Semit* 4 (1990): 72-73.

17. Aron Krochmalnik, "Das Bumsen hat nichts geändert," *Nudnik* 9 (1988): 39-40.

18. Seligmann, *Mit beschränkter Hoffnung*, 150.

19. "rah," "Jugend eines Juden im Nachkriegsdeutschland," *Oberbayerisches Volksblatt, Rosenheim*, November 8, 1988.

20. Martin Ripkens, "Zu Hause: nirgends," *Frankfurter Rundschau*, November 18, 1989.

21. Albert von Schirnding, "Romeo aus Israel," *Süddeutsche Zeitung*, November 26-27, 1988.

22. Wolfgang Görl, "Unmögliche Liebe, unmöglicher Haß," *Süddeutsche Zeitung*, November 4-5, 1988.

23. Peter Köpf, "Scheinheiligkeit bringt ihn in Rage," *Abendzeitung*, May 17, 1988.

24. Peter Köpf, "Es gibt auch jüdische Nazis," *Abendzeitung*, November 25, 1989.

25. Andrea Jahnel, "Gegen die Verdrängung," *Rheinische Post*, November 30, 1989; "rj," "Ein unbequemes Buch," *Darmstadter Echo*, November 17, 1989; Norbert Koch, "Schlechtes Gewissen?" *Die Welt*, April 30, 1988; anon., "Amüsanter Weg in die Welt der Erwachsenen," *Berliner Morgenpost*, June 17-18, 1989.

26. Eva-Elisabeth Fischer, "Der Autor für alle," *Süddeutsche Zeitung*, November 28, 1990.

118   *Notes for Pages 53–59*

27. Schalom Ben-Chorin, "Wie macht man Risches?" *Israel Nachrichten*, May 24, 1991.

28. Abi Pitum, "Subtile Weiberherrschaft," *Allgemeine Jüdische Wochenzeitung*, December 20-27, 1990.

29. Michael Zeller, "witzig—oder?" *Die Zeit*, November 16, 1990.

30. Adolf Fink, "Vom Privaten und Erotischen," *Frankfurter Allgemeine Zeitung: Beilage zur Buchmesse,* October 6, 1990; Matthias Wegner, "Drückeberger, Schürzenjäger," *Frankfurter Allgemeine Zeitung,* October 4, 1990; K. Urbach, "Ladykiller," *Münchner Merkur,* October 20, 1990; Dulore Pizzini, "Sohn liebt 'Schickse,' Mamme greift ein," *Die Presse,* March 30-31, 1991; Wolfgang Herles, "Im Schwitzkasten der Ehe," *Die Welt,* September 8, 1990; Peter Köpf, "Allein in der Badewanne," *Abendzeitung* (Munich), August 7, 1990; anon., "Schürzenjäger," *Elle* 12 (1990): 123; Günther Nenning, "Mammes, Schmock und SS," *profil* 12 (March 18, 1991): 93-94.

31. Seligmann, *Mit beschränkter Hoffnung,* 162.

32. Gertrud Koch, "Corporate identities: Zur Prosa von Dische, Biller und Seligmann," *Babylon* 7 (1990): 139-42.

33. Philip Roth, *Reading Myself and Others* (New York: Farrar, Straus and Giroux, 1975).

34. Seligmann, *Mit beschränkter Hoffnung,* 162.

35. Rafael Seligmann, "Die Juden leben," *Der Spiegel* 47 (September 1992): 75-76.

36. "Einfach eine Fehlthese?" *Der Spiegel* 49 (September 1992): 7-8.

37. Rafael Seligmann, "Unbequeme Ansichten," *Münchner Stadtzeitung,* November 5, 1988.

38. Jack Zipes, "Jewish Consciousness in Germany Today," *Telos* 93 (1992): 159-72, here, p. 171.

39. Rafael Seligmann, *Gute Nacht, Deutschland: Talkshow—Juden und Deutsche fordern: Macht endlich Schluß mit der Vergangenheit!: Schauspiel in 4 Akten* (Frankfurt am Main: S. Fischer, 1992). A puff-piece on the play by Günther Nenning, "Chronist des 4. Reiches," *Die Zeit,* April 2, 1993, attempted to create interest for its performance.

40. The biographical information and quotations are taken from a detailed interview published when her first novel appeared. See Ina Boesch, "Es gibt Menschen—und es gibt Juden," *Allgemeine jüdische Wochenzeitung,* September 8, 1989.

41. In 1978 Becker was by far the youngest of the figures interviewed. Today he stands as the most representative writer of the survivor genera-

tion in Germany. See Hans Jürgen Schultz, ed., *Mein Judentum* (Stuttgart: Kreuz, 1991), 10-18.

42. Interview with Alexandra Przyrembel on March 8, 1993, in Ithaca, New York.

43. *Anna macht Frühstück* (Munich: dtv junior, 1985). See the recent publication of her play: "Ich ziehe mir die Farben aus der Haut," *Die Palette* 9 (1993), 53-70.

44. Edgar Hilsenrath, *Zibulsky oder Antenne im Bauch* (Düsseldorf: Claasen, 1983), 11-12. (My translation.)

45. "Damit das Denken in Gang gebracht wird," *Frankfurter Rundschau*, November 8, 1988.

46. Ulrike Kolb, "Eine jüdische Geschichte," *Die Tageszeitung* (Berlin), December 3, 1988.

47. Agnes Hüfner, "Die Suche nach den Wurzeln," *Frankfurter Allgemeine Zeitung*, November 23, 1988.

48. Gabriele Winter, "Suche nach Identifikation," *Auftritt: Rhein-Main-Illustrierte*, March 1989.

49. Beatrice Eichmann-Leutnegger, "Wirrnis in Lebensmustern," *Neue Züricher Zeitung*, June 5, 1992.

50. Reinhold Horn, "Die blutrote Traumschrift," *Plärrer* (Nuremberg), June 1992.

51. Hanna Rheinz, "Bitterkraut," *Freitag* (Berlin), July 10, 1992.

52. Susanne Broos, "Wortklangfarben," *Frankfurter Rundschau*, September 26, 1992.

53. Gerhard Schulz, "Die Steppenwölfin schnuppert," *Frankfurter Allgemeine Zeitung*, May 23, 1992.

54. Patrick Süskind, *Die Taube* (Zurich: Diogenes, 1987); *Das Parfum: Die Geschichte eines Mörders* (Zurich: Diogenes, 1985); *Die Geschichte von Herrn Sommer* (Zurich: Diogenes, 1991). For the type of criticism see Katharina Reimann, "Patrick Süskinds zwei Kurzgeschichten: *Die Taube* und *Die Geschichte von Herrn Sommer*—Ein Abriß ihrer stilistischen Struktur und ihrer inhaltlichen Komponente," *Doitsubungaku Ronko* 34 (1992): 1-14. Reimann understands that the first text deals with deportation, but the Jewish subtext of both of these stories is simply lost on her.

55. Braude, *Windswept Plains*, 78.

56. Maxim Biller, "Auschwitz sehen und sterben," *Die Tempojahre* (Munich: dtv, 1991), 115-31.

Representing Jewish Sexuality

1. See Sander L. Gilman, *The Jew's Body* (New York: Routledge, 1991).

2. On the cultural background of this concept, see Jacob Katz, *Out of the Ghetto: The Social Background of Jewish Emancipation 1770-1870* (Cambridge, MA: Harvard University Press, 1973), and Rainer Erb and Werner Bergmann, *Die Nachtseite der Judenemanzipation: Der Widerstand gegen die Integration der Juden in Deutschland 1780-1860* (Berlin: Metropol, 1989).

3. Albert Drach, *Das große Protokoll gegen Zwetschkenbaum* (Munich: Carl Hanser, 1989), 20.

4. *Herr Moriz Deutschösterreicher: Eine jüdische Erzählung zwischen Assimilation und Exil*, ed. Jürgen Egyptien (Vienna: Droschl, 1988), 5.

5. Susann Heenen-Wolff, *Im Haus des Henkers: Gespräche in Deutschland* (Frankfurt am Main: Dvorah, 1992), 68-69.

6. Jacob R. Marcus, *The Colonial American Jew, 1492-1776*, 3 vols. (Detroit: Wayne State University Press, 1970), 2:984. On the American tradition, see Jay Brodbar-Nemzer, Peter Conrad, and Shelly Tenenbaum, "American Circumcision Practices and Social Reality," *Sociology and Social Research* 71 (1987): 275-79.

7. Andree, *Zur Volkskunde der Juden*, 157.

8. Humphrey Carpenter, *A Serious Character: The Life of Ezra Pound* (Boston: Houghton Mifflin, 1988), 362.

9. Richard Burton, *Love, War and Fancy: The Customs and Manners of the East from the Writings on 'The Arabian Nights,'* ed. Kenneth Walker (London: W. Kimber, 1964), 106.

10. See the exemplary use of the discussion of the Jews as a race in Richard Weinberg, "Zur Theorie einer anatomischen Rassensystematik," *Archiv für Rassen- und Gesellschafts-Biologie* 2 (1905): 198-214, especially 205-206. Weinberg notes ten different physical characteristics that determine the definition of racial difference.

11. A summary of the German Jewish views on the meaning of this practice in the 1920s can be found in the essay on "Berit mila" in the *Jüdisches Lexikon*, ed. Georg Herlitz and Bruno Kirschner, 4 vols. in 5 (Berlin: Jüdischer Verlag, 1927-30), 1:861-66. The essay stresses seven different readings of infant circumcision: as a hygienic practice, as the remains of older practices of castration, as the mark of stigmatization, as a sign of tribal membership, as a test of the child, as a sanctification of the penis, as a prophylaxis against incest. For the latter, psychoanalytic theory is evinced. On the Jewish views of the meaning and function of this practice, see J. David Bleich, *Judaism and Healing: Halakhic Perspectives* (New York: Ktav, 1981),

47-50. On the history of the Jewish tradition, see Julius Preuss, *Biblisch-talmudische Medizin: Beiträge zur Geschichte der Heilkunde und der Kultur überhaupt* (Berlin: S. Karger, 1927), 279. Compare John J. Collins, "A Symbol of Otherness: Circumcision and Salvation in the First Century," in Jacob Neusner and Ernest S. Frerichs, eds., *"To See Ourselves As Others See Us": Christians, Jews, "Others" in Late Antiquity* (Chico, CA: Scholars Press, 1985), 163-85, and Nigel Allan, "A Polish Rabbi's Circumcision Manual," *Medical History* 33 (1989): 247-54.

12. Anon. "Die rituelle Beschneidung bei den Juden und ihre Gefahren," *Journal für Kinderkrankheiten* 59 (1872): 367-72.

13. G. S. Thompson, "Circumcision—A Barbarous and Unnecessary Mutilation," *The British Medical Journal* 1 (1920): 437.

14. See in this context the most recent and most extensive American presentation of this argument: Rosemary Romberg, ed., *Circumcision: The Painful Dilemma* (South Hadley, MA: Bergin & Garvey, 1985), published in conjunction with INTACT Educational Foundation. The most recent debate in the United States about the medical implications of this widespread practice was begun by E. N. Preston, "Whither the Foreskin? A Consideration of Routine Neonatal Circumcision," *Journal of the American Medical Association* 216 (1970): 1853-58. In this vein, see also Edward Wallerstein, "Circumcision: The Uniquely American Medical Enigma," *The Urologic Clinics of North America* 12 (1985): 123-32, which discusses the debates about infection in the context of an attack on the practice. In this context, see Moisés Trachtenberg and Philip Slotkin, "Circumcision, Crucifixion, and Anti-Semitism: The Antithetical Character of Ideologies and Their Symbol Which Contain Crossed Lines," *International Review of Psycho-Analysis* 16 (1989): 459-71; E. A. Grossman and N. A. Posner, "The Circumcision Controversy: An Update," *Obstetrics and Gynecological Annual* 13 (1984): 181-95; E. Grossman and N. A. Posner, "Surgical Circumcision of Neonates: A History of Its Development," *Obstetrics and Gynecology* 58 (1981): 241-46; S. J. Waszak, "The Historic Significance of Circumcision," *Obstetrics and Gynecology* 51 (1978): 499-501.

The anthropological literature on this topic is often critical and superficial; see Desmond Morris, *Bodywatching* (London: Jonathan Cape, 1985), 218-20. By far the best anthropological discussion of the meaning of the circumcised body is in the published work of James Boon: *Other Tribes, Other Scribes* (New York: Cambridge University Press, 1982), 162-68; *Affinities and Extremes* (Chicago: University of Chicago Press, 1990), 55-60; see also his unpublished paper "Circumscribing Circumcision/Uncircumcision" (1990), in which the meaning of the act of circumcision is most intelligently and most sophisticatedly called into question. The reading of the Jewish practice in the light of the history of nineteenth-century anthropology is extraordinarily well documented in Howard Eilberg-Schwartz, *The Savage in Judaism: An Anthropology of Israelite Reli-*

gion and Ancient Judaism (Bloomington: Indiana University Press, 1990), 141-76. On the religious reading of circumcision within Rabbinic Judaism, see Daniel Boyarin, "'This We Know to Be the Carnal Israel': Circumcision and the Erotic Life of God and Israel," *Critical Inquiry* 18 (1992): 474-506, as well as his *Carnal Israel: Reading Sex in Talmudic Culture* (Berkeley: University of California Press, 1993). See also Moisés Trachtenberg, *Psicanálise da circuncisão* (Porto Alegre: Sagra, 1990), and Claude Lévi-Strauss, "Exode sur Exode," *Homme* 28 (1988): 106-107.

15. See my essay "Jewish Writers and German Letters: Anti-Semitism and the Hidden Language of the Jews," *The Jewish Quarterly Review* 77 (1986/7): 119-48.

16. Jakov Lind, the Viennese Jewish novelist, long a resident of Great Britain, stated it most clearly in his autobiography, *Counting My Steps: An Autobiography* (London: Macmillan, 1969), 135-36:

All he needed was a foreskin,
otherwise he felt all right.
He lived it up like a Duke in his castle,
with pheasant shooting and old paintings,
all he needed was a little foreskin,
otherwise he was all right.

He lived it up like the Roi de Soleil
in Trianon, they feed him oysters with a spoon,
all he needed was a bit of skin,
otherwise he was all right.

He lived it up like Zeus in the Parthenon,
makes it only with Goddesses,
all he needs is a bit more skin
and everything will be fine.

17. On the colonial implications of the debate about circumcision in Great Britain and its association with Islam as well as with the Jews, see Ronald Hyam, *Empire and Sexuality: The British Experience* (Manchester: Manchester University Press, 1990), 76-79.

18. There is no comprehensive study of the German debates on circumcision. See Julius Preuss, "Die Beschneidung nach Bibel und Talmud," *Wiener klinische Rundschau* 11 (1897): 708-709, 724-27; J. Alkvist, "Geschichte der Circumcision," *Janus* 30 (1926): 86-104, 152-71, as well as Samuel Krauss, *Geschichte der jüdischen Ärzte vom frühsten Mittelalter bis zur Gleichberechtigung* (Vienna: A. S. Bettelheim-Stiftung, 1930), 157-58.

19. At least one Jewish convert to Christianity in the sixteenth century, Antonius Margaritha, while stressing the evident pain of the infant, does not condemn the ritual practice. See his *Der gantz Jüdisch glaub*

(Augsburg: Heinrich Steyner, 1530), H1v-H2r. On Margaritha, see my *Jewish Self-Hatred: Anti-Semitism and the Hidden Language of the Jews* (Baltimore: Johns Hopkins University Press, 1986), 62-66.

20. The authorized German editions of Mantegazza are: *Die Physiologie der Liebe*, trans. Eduard Engel (Jena: Hermann Costenoble, 1877); *Die Hygiene der Liebe*, trans. R. Teutscher (Jena: Hermann Costenoble, [1877]); *Anthropologisch-kulturhistorische Studien über die Geschlechtsverhältnisse des Menschen* (Jena: Hermann Costenoble, [1891]).

21. On Mantegazza, see Giovanni Landucci, *Darwinismo a Firenze: Tra scienza e ideologia (1860-1900)* (Florence: Leo S. Olschki, 1977), 107-28.

22. The relevant passages in the German edition, *Anthropologisch-kulturhistorische Studien*, are on pages 132-37. All of the quotations from Mantegazza are from the English translation: Paolo Mantegazza, *The Sexual Relations of Mankind*, trans. Samuel Putnam (New York: Eugenics Publishing, 1938).

23. Spinoza's text, often cited and often commented on in the nineteenth century, labels circumcision as the primary reason for the survival of the Jews as "they have incurred universal hatred by cutting themselves off completely from all other peoples." It also made them "effeminate" and, thus, unlikely to assume a political role in the future. Benedict Spinoza, *The Political Works*, trans. A. G. Wernham (Oxford: Oxford University Press, 1958), 63.

24. Mantegazza, *Sexual Relations*, 99.

25. Edward Westermarck, *The History of Human Marriage*, 3 vols. (London: Macmillan, 1921), 1:561.

26. Mantegazza, *Sexual Relations*, 98.

27. Mantegazza, *Sexual Relations*, 98-99.

28. August Forel, *Die sexuelle Frage* (Munich: Ernst Reinhardt, 1906), 172; *The Sexual Question*, trans. C. F. Marshall (New York: Medical Art Agency, 1922), 158. Forel cites Edward Westermarck as his authority.

29. William Osler, "Israel and Medicine" (1914), in William Osler, *Men and Books*, ed. Earl F. Nation (Pasadena, CA: Castle Press, 1959), 56.

30. Ernest Crawley, *The Mystic Rose: A Study of Primitive Marriage* (London: Macmillan, 1902), 138.

31. Anatole Leroy-Beaulieu, *Israel among the Nations: A Study of the Jews and Antisemitism*, trans. Frances Hellman (New York: G. P. Putnam's Sons, 1895), 229.

32. *Theodor Gomperz: ein Gelehrtenleben im Bürgertum der Franz-Josefs-Zeit: Auswahl seiner Briefe und Aufzeichnungen, 1869-1912*, ed.

Robert A. Kann (Vienna: Verlag der Österreichischen Akademie der Wissenschaften, 1974), 226.

33. J. H. F. Autenrieth, *Abhandlung über den Ursprung der Beschneidung* (Tübingen: Heinrich Laupp, 1829).

34. John Lubbock, *The Origin of Civilization and the Primitive Condition of Man* (1870; repr. Chicago: University of Chicago Press, 1978), 237.

35. Lubbock, *Origin of Civilization*, 243.

36. Dr. Hacker, "Die Beschneidung der Juden, ein Überrest der Barbarei dieses Volkes, und ein Ersatz für seine früheren Menschenopfer," *Medicinischer Argos* 5 (1843): 375-79.

37. Wilhelm Wundt, *Elements of Folk Psychology: Outlines of a Psychological History of the Development of Mankind*, trans. Edward Leroy Schaub (London: George Allen & Unwin, 1916), 445.

38. Wundt, *Elements*, 498.

39. *Philo*, trans. F. H. Colson (Cambridge, MA: Harvard University Press, 1953-63), 7:103-105 (*De specialibus legibus*, 1: 4-7). See Theodore James, "Philo on Circumcision," *South African Medical Journal* 50 (1976): 1409-12.

40. Roy S. Wolper, "Circumcision as Polemic in the Jew Bill of 1753: The Cutter Cut?" *Eighteenth-Century Life* 7 (1982): 28-36.

41. See my *Sexuality: An Illustrated History* (New York: Wiley, 1989).

42. Samuel Holdheim, *Über die Beschneidung zunächst in religiös-dogmatischer Beziehung* (Schwerin: C. Kürschner, 1844).

43. J. Bergson, *Die Beschneidung vom historischen, kritischen und medizinischen Standpunkt* (Berlin: Th. Scherk/Athenaeum, 1844).

44. Dr. Wolfers, "Ueber die Beschneidung der Judenkinder," *Zeitschrift für Staatsarzneikunde* 9 (1825): 205-209.

45. See the discussion in M. G. Salomon, *Die Beschneidung, historisch und medizinisch beleuchtet* (Braunschweig: Vieweg, 1844).

46. Dr. Klein, "Die rituelle Circumcision, eine sanitätspolizeiliche Frage," *Allgemeine Medizinische Central-Zeitung* 22 (1853): 368-69.

47. S. Arnhold, *Die Beschneidung und ihre Reform* (Leipzig: n.p., 1847), 50-51.

48. Lea Fleischmann's work provides an account of growing up as a Jewish girl and woman in Germany in *Dies ist nicht mein Land: Eine Jüdin verläßt die Bundesrepublik* (Hamburg: Hoffman und Campe, 1980), and in her account of her early days in Israel as an adult, *Ich bin Israelin: Erfahrung in einem orientalischen Land* (Hamburg: Hoffman and Campe, 1982); see also

her two volumes of short stories, *Nichts ist so, wie es uns scheint: Jüdische Geschichten* (Hamburg: Rasch und Röhring, 1985) and *Abrahams Heimkehr: Geschichten zu den jüdischen Feiertagen* (Hamburg: Rasch und Röhring, 1989). In all these contexts, male writers evoke the question of their sexual identity. Barbara Honigmann's *Roman von einem Kind* (Frankfurt am Main: Luchterhand, 1989), which is actually six interconnected tales, also represents early childhood awareness without analogous attention to the politics of the body.

49. Esther Dischereit, *Joëmis Tisch: Eine jüdische Geschichte* (Frankfurt am Main: Suhrkamp, 1988), 11.

50. Holland is the daughter of a Communist, Jewish father and a non-Jewish, Polish mother. The complexity of this for her own identity is outlined in a profile of her by Roger Cohen, "Holland without a Country," *New York Times Magazine*, August 8, 1993, 28-32. Schlomo Perel, *Korim li Shelomoh Perel* (Tel Aviv: Yediot aharonot / Sifre hemed, 1991).

51. Irene Dische, *Fromme Lügen*, trans. Otto Bayer and Monika Elwenspoek (Frankfurt am Main: Eichborn, 1989), 5-75. See also her *Der Doktor braucht ein Heim*, trans. Reinhard Kaiser (Frankfurt am Main: Suhrkamp, 1990). Her most recent novel deals with the question of the ill male body with AIDS; see *Ein fremdes Gefühl oder Veränderungen über einen Deutschen*, trans. Reinhard Kaiser (Berlin: Rowohlt, 1993). Unless noted, all translations are mine.

52. Jane E. Gilbert, *Ich mußte mich vom Haß befreien: Eine Jüdin emigriert nach Deutschland* (Bern: Scherz, 1989), 204. Unless noted, all translations are mine.

53. Susan Nieman, *Slow Fire: Jewish Notes from Berlin* (New York: Schocken Books, 1992), ix. References are to the uncorrected galleys. On the book, see James E. Ponet, "German Past Imperfect," *Tikkun* 8 (March/April 1993): 61.

54. Doris Dörrie, *Love, Pain and the Whole Damn Thing*, trans. John E. Woods (New York: Viking, 1989), 35-36. (The original is titled *Liebe, Schmerz und das ganze verdammte Zeug* [Zurich: Diogenes, 1987]).

55. All references are to the unaltered reprint of the novel the following year: Rafael Seligmann, *Rubinsteins Versteigerung* (Frankfurt am Main: Eichborn, 1989). Unless noted, all translations are mine. For the prior publishing history of the novel, see Henryk M. Broder, "Rubinsteins Beschwerden," *Die Zeit*, August 18, 1989, 13.

56. Elvira Grözinger, "Zwischen Exhibitionismus und Literatur: Von den Debütanden Seligmann, Biller, Dische und dem kleinen Unterschied," *Semit* 4 (1990): 72-73.

57. All references are to *Bronsteins Kinder* (Frankfurt am Main: Suhrkamp, 1986). Unless noted, all translations are mine.

58. Edgar Hilsenrath, *The Nazi and the Barber* (New York: Manor, 1973). The English translation appeared four years before the original German, which was published in 1977.

59. Edgar Hilsenrath, *Jossel Wassermanns Heimkehr* (Munich: Piper, 1993), 282.

60. Hannelore Schlaffer, "Mit dem entlarvenden Blick einer Göre: Die neue literarische Jugendkultur oder: Ihr Phänotyp Maxim Biller," *Frankfurter Rundschau*, August 28, 1992.

61. Maxim Biller, *Wenn ich einmal reich und tot bin* (Cologne: Kiepenheuer und Witsch, 1990), 18.

62. Gilman, *The Jew's Body*, 205-207.

63. Andreas Sinakowski, *Das Verhör* (Berlin: Basisdruck, 1991).

64. Robert Schindel, *Gebürtig* (Frankfurt am Main: Suhrkamp, 1992). Unless noted, all translations are mine. See also his *Die Nacht der Harlekine* (Frankfurt am Main: Suhrkamp, 1994).

65. Simon Louvish, *The Therapy of Avram Blok: A Phantasm of Israel among the Nations* (London: Flamingo, 1990), 143. Unexpurgated version of the original novel, published in 1985. On the childhood memory of the anxiety about being circumcised in Prague, see Peter Finkelgruen, *Haus Deutschland oder Die Geschichte eines ungesühnten Mordes* (Reinbek bei Hamburg: Rowohlt, 1994), 21-23. On the fictionalization of the meaning of the uncircumcised Jew after the Shoah, see the Hungarian novelist György Dalos, *Die Beschneidung,* trans. György Dalos and Elsbeth Zylla (Frankfurt am Main: Suhrkamp, 1993).

66. Dan Jacobson, *The God-Fearer* (London: Bloomsbury, 1992), 60.

67. Erich Wulffen, *Der Sexualverbrecher* (Berlin: P. Langenscheidt, 1910), 302. This was considered to be one of the major innovative contributions to the criminology of the day. See the review in the *Jahrbuch für sexuelle Zwischenstufen*, NF 3 (1911): 376-78.

68. John S. Billings, "Vital Statistics of the Jews," *North American Review* 153 (1891): 84.

69. All of these fin-de-siècle sources are cited by Havelock Ellis, *Studies in the Psychology of Sex* (Philadelphia: F. A. Davis, 1900-28), 5:185-86.

70. Hanns Sachs, *Freud: Master and Friend* (Cambridge, MA: Harvard University Press, 1946), 19.

71. Leopold Löwenfeld, *Über die sexuelle Konstitution und andere Sexualprobleme* (Wiesbaden: J. F. Bergmann, 1911), 75-76.

72. *Protokolle der Wiener Psychoanalytischen Vereinigung,* ed. Herman Nunberg and Ernst Federn, 4 vols. (Frankfurt am Main: Fischer, 1976-81),

2:41; translation by M. Nunberg, from *Minutes of the Vienna Psychoanalytic Society,* 4 vols. (New York: International Universities Press, 1962-75), 2:45.

73. Alice Miller, *Banished Knowledge: Facing Childhood Injuries,* trans. Leila Vennewitz (New York: Doubleday, 1990), 135-39; the emphasis is hers. See Lawrence Birken, "From Seduction Theory to Oedipus Complex: A Historical Analysis," *New German Critique* 43 (1988): 83-96.

74. Morris, *Bodywatching,* 218-20.

75. All of the following quotations are taken from Miller, *Banished Knowledge,* 135-43.

76. See the discussion of Erikson in my *Difference and Pathology: Stereotypes of Sexuality, Race, and Madness* (Ithaca, NY: Cornell University Press, 1985), 31-32.

77. See, in this context, Susann Heenen-Wolff, "Les travaux de Freud sur Moïse et sa relation au judaïsme et à l'antisémitisme," *Le Coq-Héron* 120 (1991): 9-17; David Bakan, "A Note on Freud's Idea that Moses was an Egyptian as Scriptural and Traditional," *Journal of the History of the Behavioral Sciences* 25 (1989): 163-64; Ritchie Robertson, "Freud's Testament: *Moses and Monotheism,*" in Edward Timms and Naomi Segal, eds., *Freud in Exile* (New Haven: Yale University Press, 1988), 80-89; Michael P. Carroll, "*Moses and Monotheism* and the Psychoanalytic Study of Early Christian Mythology," *Journal of Psychohistory* 15 (1988): 295-310; Philip Rieff, "Intimations of Therapeutic Truth: Decoding Appendix G in *Moses and Monotheism,*" *Humanities in Society* 4 (1981): 197-201; Jean Jofen, "A Freudian Interpretation of Freud's *Moses and Monotheism,*" *Michigan Academician* 12 (1979-80): 231-40; Edwin R. Wallace IV, "The Psychodynamic Determinants of *Moses and Monotheism,*" *Psychiatry* 40 (1977): 79-87; M. S. Bergmann, "Moses and the Evolution of Freud's Jewish Identity," *Israeli Annals of Psychiatry* 14 (1976): 3-26.

78. Heschel, "Jüdisch-feministische Theologie und Antijudaismus," 54-103.

79. "Völkische Stimmen," *Der Spiegel* 29 (November 1979): 46.

80. Clive Sinclair, "The Promised Land," *Hearts of Gold* (London: Allison & Busby, 1979), 27.

81. See my essay "The Indelibility of Circumcision," *Koroth* (Jerusalem) 9 (1991): 806-17.

82. *Der Spiegel* 4 (April 1992): 41-50.

Index

SANDER L. GILMAN is Professor of German, History of Science, Psychiatry and Jewish Studies at the University of Chicago. A cultural and literary historian, he is the author or editor of over forty books. His most recent books include *Freud, Race, and Gender* and *The Case of Sigmund Freud.* Other works include *Seeing the Insane, Inscribing the Other, Difference and Pathology: Stereotypes of Sexuality, Race, and Madness,* and *Jewish Self-Hatred: Anti-Semitism and the Hidden Language of the Jews.*